Lighting Spaces

Lighting Spaces

Roger Yee

Visual Reference Publications Inc., New York

Left: Morongo Casino, Resort & Spa, Cabazon, California. **Lighting Design:** Visual Terrain, Inc. **Architecture:** The Jerde Partnership, Thalden-Boyd. **Photography:** Tom Paiva.

Lighting Spaces

GROUP PUBLISHER — Larry Fuersich
larry@visualreference.com

PUBLISHER — Bill Ash
bill@visualreference.com

EDITORIAL DIRECTOR — Roger Yee
yeerh@aol.com

CREATIVE ART DIRECTOR — Veronika Cherepanina
veronika@visualreference.com

PRODUCTION MANAGER — John Hogan
johnhvrp@yahoo.com

CIRCULATION MANAGER — Amy Yip
amy@visualreference.com

MARKETING COORDINATOR — Nika Chopra
nika@visualreference.com

CONTROLLER — Angie Goulimis
angie@visualreference.com

Visual Reference Publications, Inc.

302 Fifth Avenue
New York, NY 10001
Tel: 212.279.7000 • Fax: 212.279.7014

www.visualreference.com

Distributors to the trade in the United States and Canada
Watson-Guptill
770 Broadway
New York, NY 10003

Distributors outside the United States and Canada
HarperCollins International
10 East 53rd Street
New York, NY 10022-5299

Library of Congress Cataloging in Publication Data:
Lighting Spaces

Printed in China

ISBN: 978-1-58471-116-2
ISBN: 1-58471-116-7

Book Design: Veronika Cherepanina

light

www.artemide.us

systems

Artemide®
ARCHITECTURAL

ECOTECTURAL
Architectural lighting for sustainable design.

I AM SUSTAINABLE.

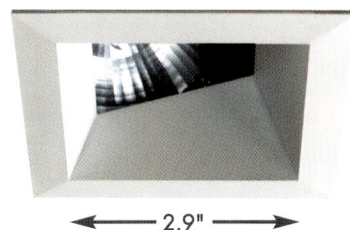

← 2.9" →

I AM AMERLUX.

Contents

Introduction

Turn on the Lights!

What does Old McDonald see when he peers into the nighttime sky?

Every city or town dweller knows the initial shock of viewing the starry canopy over the countryside. Evening in a modern urban landscape is so bright it routinely masks the splendors of the universe. However, there's nothing like a being caught in a power blackout to demonstrate how much electric lighting has changed our lives since Thomas Edison invented the incandescent lamp in 1879.

Nightlife, once celebrated in art as a source of danger, romance, confusion and supernatural phenomena, has become an indispensable way to extend daytime economic activities and intensify evening recreational pursuits--to the point that many Americans fail to get enough sleep. In fact, one in five adults in the United States currently suffers from daytime sleepiness, and 50 percent of those aged 18 to 34 say daytime sleepiness interferes with their work. Much of the credit goes to professional lighting designers for making the built environment so compelling that we perform our occupations with acuity and enthusiasm during the day, and ignore our natural circadian rhythms as night falls to keep working or playing.

One basic measure of lighting's importance is the volume of energy Americans devote to it. Energy consumption for all lighting in the United States, according to a 2002 study for the Department of Energy, is estimated to be 8.2 quads (one quad equals 10^{15} BTUs), 765 TWh/yr (terawatt-hours per year) or about 22 percent of total electricity generated. Sector by sector, aggregate energy usage for lighting breaks down into residential at 27 percent, commercial at 51 percent, industrial at 14 percent, and outdoor stationary at 8 percent. For the two largest sectors, commercial and residential, lighting constitutes approximately 17.6 percent of total building energy consumption or some 30.3 percent of total building electricity use.

But another, equally dramatic sign of lighting's role in modern life is its growing use not merely to illuminate tasks but to influence perception. Of course, a surprising number of offices, hotels, courthouses, hospitals, restaurants, schools, convention centers and the like continues to embrace mediocre construction illuminated by nondescript lighting. Increasingly, however, the public is encountering unique environments envisioned by major architects and interior designers with help from lighting designers, in which the lighting is critical to the powerful inspirational message of the commercial or institutional space.

Professional lighting design at its best does more than enable us to accomplish whatever activities draw us to a space, indoors or outdoors. It adds meaning to whatever we do. The artistry and technology that today's lighting designers bring to bear on architecture and interior design is impressively displayed in the following pages of Lighting Spaces, where these talented individuals and organizations come with names, skills, talents and portfolios that make our days and nights worth seeing.

Roger Yee
Editor

Project: Yale University Art Gallery Renovation, New Haven, CT
Original Building Architect: Louis Kahn
Original Building Lighting Design: Richard Kelly
Renovation Architect: Polshek Partnership Architects
Renovation Lighting Design: Fisher Marantz Stone
Exhibition Lighting Design: Hefferan Partnership Lighting Design
Lighting Manufacturer: Lighting Services Inc

Ann Kale Associates Ltd.

1569 San Leandro Lane
Santa Barbara, CA 93108
805.969.7660
805.969.7663 (Fax)
www.annkale.com

Ann Kale Associates Ltd.

Memorable guest experiences are expected from leading hotels and restaurants and Ann Kale Associates works closely with hospitality clients to make the most of each project. Consider four recent projects. Per se, famed-chef Thomas Keller's New York restaurant is elegant dining at its best. Lighting throughout accentuates Tihany Design's rich furnishings and bronze floor while providing complementary lighting to the patrons themselves. In Tihany Design's Club Prive at Bellagio, in Las Vegas, low, seductive lighting lets players relax in semi-privacy, amidst mahogany and glass panels and plush seating, at blackjack tables under recessed accentlights. At The Sea Grill, another project with Tihany Design in New York's Rockefeller Center, guests viewing the fabled winter ice rink and summer garden find their visit enriched by light filtering through a custom

1, 4: **per se,** New York, New York, Tihany Design, interior designer; Paul Warchol, photographer.

2, 3: **Club Prive,** Bellagio, Las Vegas, Nevada, Tihany Design, interior designer; Andrea Martiradonna, photographer.

Ann Kale Associates Ltd.

Hospitality

glass curtain, blue resin sheets, and sand-blasted glass panels, evoking the sea's changing moods. At Suba Ann Kale Associates and Ardre Kikoski Architect transformed a 1909 tenement storefront and basement into one of New York City's most unique restaurants. The lower level concrete dining platform is surrounded by a moat where concealed underwater fixtures gently bathe brick walls in shimmering dancing waves of light.

1, 2, 3: The Sea Grill, New York, New York, Tihany Design, interior designer; Paul Warchol, photographer.

4, 5, 6: Suba, New York, New York, Andrea Kikoski Architect, architect; Peter Aaron/Esto Photographics, photographer.

Ann Kale Associates Ltd.

Historic

Can modern lighting let us see the past anew? While refurbished original decorative lighting fixtures can provide much of the illumination for restored historic buildings, such as the 1906 Essex County Courthouse, in Newark, New Jersey, originally designed by architect Cass Gilbert, they may not suffice to meet contemporary lighting standards. Farewell, Mills and Gatsch Architects recently worked with Ann Kale Associates as lighting designer to return the landmark, four-story, 120,000-square-foot Courthouse, featuring an atrium and central stair connecting three levels of courtrooms beneath three Tiffany skylight domes, to its former splendor. New lighting methods and technologies enabled Ann Kale Associates to increase illumination levels and highlight decorative forms and surfaces without disturbing the original architecture. The once dark stairs, for example, are now illuminated by a series of miniature fiber-optic accents lights recessed into the cornice below the Tiffany skylights. Courtrooms are properly illuminated for the first time by a combination of restored decorative fixtures and recessed miniature downlights concealed within ceiling coves, molding and beams. Where possible, once closed skylights are restored to provide daylight. The result is a magnificent Beaux Arts building with award-winning lighting (IES Lumen West Award of Excellence, IIDA Award of Merit, New Jersey Historic Preservation Award) that revives and even enhances its heritage.

1 - 5: Essex County Courthouse, Newark, New Jersey, Farewell, Mills and Gatsch Architects, architect; Brian Rose, photographer.

Ann Kale Associates Ltd.

Corporate

Lighting's primary role in corporate facilities is to help architects and interior designers create superior workplaces for accurate, reliable and cost-effective operations. However, many businesses must also consider public image, especially at such conspicuous locations as corporate headquarters, giving lighting a broader assignment to portray their organizations to the public. This is the strategy Computer Science Corporation pursued at its new corporate headquarters in Austin, designed by Page Southerland Page, architect, with Ann Kale Associates as lighting designer. Inside the 7,500-square-foot ground floor lobby, the lighting design has produced a luminous environment with glowing glass walls that extends a simple, coolly modern greeting to employees and visitors alike. The effect comes from back lighting each glass panel with a row of halogen strip lights at the top and bottom of eight-inch deep cavities, and spotlighting furniture groupings with track-mounted overhead halogen lights placed above a metal grid ceiling. On the exterior façade, a series of wall-mounted sconces that hold four metal halide lamps apiece, two aiming up to dramatize the rough-cut limestone columns and two aiming down to illuminate the sidewalk, establish a dignified and attractive presence for the building in the community, laying a solid foundation for corporate citizenship.

1 - 4: Computer Science Corporation, Austin, Texas, Page Southerland Page, architect; Tim Griffith, Paul Bardagiy, photographers.

Ann Kale Associates Ltd.

Academic

Educational facilities demand a diversity of lighting solution to illuminate environments ranging from classrooms to stadiums. A typical example is the lighting designed by Ann Kale Associates for the new 43,000 sq. ft. K.C. Irving Environmental Science Center at Acadia University, Wolfville, Nova Scotia, Canada, designed by Robert A.M. Stern Architects. The university required that only energy efficient, long life sustainable sources be used. The architects required that minimal recessed fixtures be used and that the lighting appear to be incandescent. The solution proved to be a series of custom designed compact fluorescent chandeliers, pendants and wall sconces with custom amber tinted glass diffused shades, all carefully studied with the use of computer

calculations. In the Garden Room, for example, fluorescent custom chandeliers, uplit barrel-vault coffered ceiling and table lamps provide students with a beautiful environmentally sustainable space to relax, socialize, work on laptops or read. The conference room incorporates a fluorescent lit lay-light ceiling to provide ample illumination for video conferencing high foot candle requirements. The auditorium uses a combination of fluorescent decorative fixtures and halogen downlights to accommodate the 1 to 30 foot candle range. Throughout the project Ann Kale Associates was able to conceal high tech solutions within traditionally decorative elements.

1 - 4: Acadia University, K.C. Irving Environmental Science Center, Wolfville, Nova Scotia, Canada, Robert A.M. Stern Architects, architect; Peter Aaron/Esto Photographics, photographer.

AWA Architectural Lighting Designers

504 LaGuardia Place #5
New York, NY 10012
212.473.9797
212.473.9708 (Fax)

12 Shubhada
Sir Pochkhanwala Road
Worli
Mumbai 400 030, India

69 Jervois Street
Suite 1105
Sheung Wan
Hong Kong SAR, China

newyork@awalightingdesigners.com
www.awalightingdesigners.com

mumbai@awalightingdesigners.com

hongkong@awalightingdesigners.com

AWA Architectural Lighting Designers
Commercial and Institutional

If using lighting to shape a commercial or institutional facility, relate it to its setting, and produce quality workplace and nighttime illumination sounds complicated, it is. AWA Architectural Lighting Designers considers the architect's intent and the project's inherent structure, classifying it into pieces whose key features can be highlighted, and examining viewing angles and enclosures. Then, the firm examines the facility's surrounding neighborhood to discern its character and the impact of nighttime lighting. If the facility is large and complex, lighting can create a visual hierarchy to guide people through, with focused lighting augmenting circulation patterns, providing wayfinding cues, and highlighting points of interest, and diffuse lighting establishing an overall tone and feeling. Importantly, the firm concentrates on contrast engineering, because what we see is largely affected by the contrast between surfaces and materials. Although such lamps as fluorescents and HIDs are generally selected for high lumen efficiency and long lamp life, along with low-voltage incandescent and miniaturized metal halide lamps for focal points, impact daylighting and may require control systems that adjust electric lighting to time of day or natural lighting levels, keeping the interior in touch with the natural world.

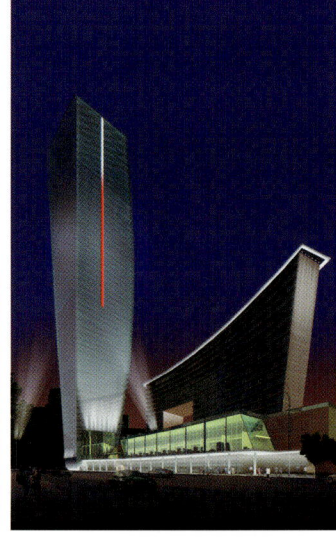

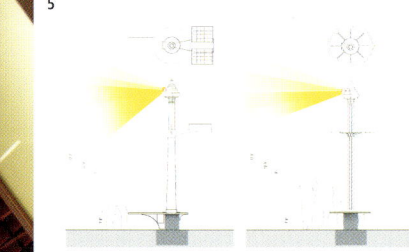

1, 4, 6: Peak Tower, Hong Kong, China, Ronald Lu & Partners, architect; Marcel Lam, photographer.

2, 3: The Courtyard, Mumbai, India, KSDC, architect; Abhay Wadhwa, photographer.

5: Hampi Temple, India, Fixture design prototype.

7: U Bora Tower, Dubai, UAE, Aedas, architect;

8: Windsor Tower Complex, Mumbai, India, Architect Hafeez Contractor, architect; Abhay Wadhwa, photographer.

AWA Architectural Lighting Designers

At the vast scale of civic or transportation structures—such as courthouses, airports, bridges, tunnels, historic buildings, or libraries—rooting them in their cultural and physical context is particularly relevant in lighting them. For this reason, AWA Architectural Lighting Designers and the architect, engineer, and/or client jointly consider how to best understand each project's vision, setting, and relationship to its community. Because multiple stakeholders are routinely involved, including government agencies and local residents as well as the project team, consensus building and a roadmap founded in research and experience are mandatory. In the process, the architect's intent, the inherent organization of the structure and its key features, the viewing angles and such external factors as wind speed, vibration, weather patterns, and safety and maintenance requirements must all be acknowledged. Such practical concerns are also reflected in the choice of equipment, requiring energy-efficient, long-life lamps such as metal halides, and maintenance-friendly, easy-access fixtures. Color is likewise used pragmatically to guide drivers or pedestrians by accenting or defining particular areas. Both daylighting and nightlighting must be closely studied to evaluate energy conservation, environmental impact, light pollution, and light trespass, issues that cannot be ignored when a structure of monumental significance is being illuminated.

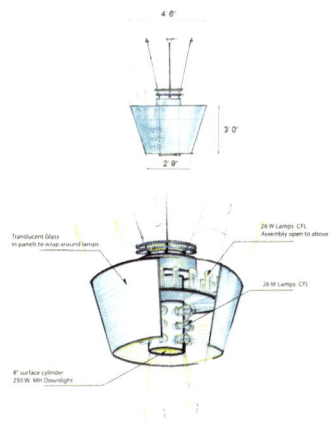

2: Peak Tower, Tram Station, Hong Kong, China, Ronald Lu & Partners, architect; Marcel Lam, photographer.

3: Peak Tower, Escalators, Hong Kong, China, Ronald Lu & Partners, architect; Marcel Lam, photographer.

4, 6: Port Authority Bus Terminal, Lobbies, New York, New York, Beyer Blinder Belle, architect.

1: Bayonne Bridge, Bayonne, New Jersey, Vanderweil Engineers, engineer; Abhay Wadhwa, photographer.

5: Mumbai University, Convocation Hall, Mumbai, India, Abha Narain Lambah Associates, architect; Abhay Wadhwa, photographer.

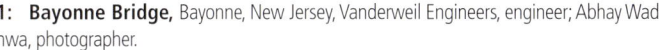

AWA Architectural Lighting Designers

Exterior and Landscape

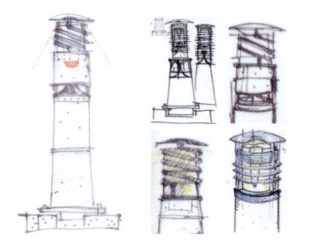

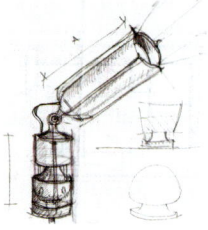

The resemblance between exterior and landscape lighting and stage lighting is close, with certain elements brought to the forefront and others playing secondary or tertiary roles. In its exteriors and landscape lighting projects, AWA Architectural Lighting Designers finds that these elements have interlocking relationships, supporting and highlighting the most critical elements identified by clients. Effective lighting calls for exploration of the setting and environment to understand the foliage, seasons, usage and surrounding environs. In addition, the environmental implications of the lighting should be considered, such as possible angles and views, neighborhood impact, nighttime lighting consequences, and shadow management. The choice of equipment reflects a long-term view, with lamps embracing energy efficiency, long lamp life, easy installation and low maintenance, and luminaires accounting for such variables as materials, fastening hardware, marine environment, flexibility, movement, and optical distribution. Color selection is also seen in context, sympathizing with the setting and guiding viewers towards specific directions or destinations. Not surprisingly, daylighting takes on a special importance in exteriors and landscape. AWA produces sun studies to replicate natural lighting patterns whenever possible. If the outcome does not precisely replicate the sun, it creates impressive facsimiles nonetheless.

1: Peak Tower, Hong Kong, China, Ronald Lu & Partners, architect; Marcel Lam, photographer.

2: Mantri Altius, Bangalore, India, RSP Architects Pvt. Ltd., architect; Abhay Wadhwa, photographer.

3: 3 West 13th Street, New York, New York, Avi Oster, architect; John Bartelstone, photographer.

4: Light/Speaker, Fixture design prototype.

5, 6: Mumbai University, Convocation Hall, Mumbai, India, Abha Narain Lambah Associates, architect; Abhay Wadhwa, photographer.

AWA Architectural Lighting Designers

Retail

It's not for sale. Nevertheless, lighting plays a major role in a retail facility, enhancing the shopping experience defined by the client, customers, architect and/or interior designer to attract customers into the store, feature merchandise, and promote sales. In the lighting environments designed by AWA Architectural Lighting Designers, lighting also makes customers feel desirable, energetic and eager to shop. How does the firm stay on retailing's cutting edge, where many of its clients operate mid-range and high-end boutiques, while increasing the range of its work? Besides maintaining a comprehensive design materials library, it studies the brand attributes of clients' labels and companies in depth, analyzing the messages they convey to consumers. Once a client's use of space is determined, appropriate lighting can be devised. AWA Architectural Lighting Designers treats the four key retail areas—sales floor, show windows, ancillary space and exterior space—as interdependent elements of one stage, choosing its approach and equipment with great care. Such lamps as metal halide, LEDs, and fiber optics are combined with a broad range of luminaires, from custom-designed pendants to railing lights, and colors and tones that complement people, reinforce themes, and highlight merchandise, all producing a satisfying shopping experience and inspiring return visits.

1: Joy Shoes, Mumbai, India, Kavita Sarathy Architects, architect; Abhay Wadhwa, photographer.

2: Peak Tower, Hong Kong, China, Ronald Lu & Partners, architect; Marcel Lam, photographer.

3: Vaibhav Mall, Vishakapatnam, India, Conceptual Rendering.

4: KI Furniture Showroom, Chicago, Illinois, Cecil, Pierce & Associates, architect; Cecil, Pierce & Associates, photographer.

5: Aqous Showroom, New York, New York, Sebastian Agneesens, interior designer; Abhay Wadhwa, photographer.

AWA Architectural Lighting Designers
Hospitality

Why do customers gravitate towards certain hospitality environments and return time after time? It's no coincidence when a restaurant, hotel or lounge projects a specific sense of place, enables customers to look good, and displays a high level of energy. For AWA Architectural Lighting Designers, the primary goal in designing hospitality lighting environments is to facilitate the customer experience by working closely with the architect, interior designer and/or client, considering the desired mood, size of groups accommodated, and hours of operations. To maintain a creative edge, the firm maintains an extensive design materials library. To light a specific space, it typically uses ambient lighting at focal points with up and downlighting options. Incandescents and low-voltage halogens are specified frequently, but fluorescent and miniature HIDs can be chosen along with such new emerging technologies as LEDs, LEPs, and fiber optics for their special properties. A broad range of fixtures, from custom-designed pendant lights to lighting built into architectural elements, exploit the characteristics of the space and the theme being evoked. Color can complement the perception of people, food and things, and reinforce themes simultaneously. Whatever the approach, hospitality lighting environments designed by AWA Architectural Lighting Designers encourages customers to return—time and time again.

1, 2: BLVD, New York, New York, ETB Restaurant Group, interior designer; Abhay Wadhwa, photographer.

3, 5, 6: Ludo, New York, New York, Post Logic Studio, interior designer; Matthew Clowney, photographer.

4: Furusato Restaurant, Macao, China, Chhada & Siembieda Designers, architect; Abhay Wadhwa, photographer.

7: BrickLane, New York, New York, AWA, interior designer; Abhay Wadhwa, photographer.

8: Crash Mansion, New York, New York, ETB Restaurant Group, interior designer; Jeff Johnson, photographer.

23

AWA Architectural Lighting Designers

Residential

After the architect establishes a vision for a residence, AWA Architectural Lighting Designers creates a lighting scheme reflecting that vision, just as it would for any other space—with one major difference. Residential work is personal in nature, reflecting a family's tastes and styles. AWA takes the charge very seriously. So, besides creating the ambience, the firm investigates such practical issues as the longevity and durability of lamps and fixtures. Lighting must accommodate the specific function behind each public or private space, as well as the family's character and preferences. AWA's nuanced approach to design combines concealed and built-in fixtures with "symbolic candles" such as pendants, sconces and actual candles to provide visible sources of light. Though incandescents and low-voltage halogens are the two lamps most commonly used, they can work with a broad range of fixtures, using colors that lean towards additive pigmentation to augment the colors of materials and furnishings. AWA also designs with daylight to see how space will appear under electric lighting in four light settings: morning and daytime, evening/dusk, nighttime and sleep. Does residential lighting warrant this much attention? Ask the families served by the firm.

1, 7: Hahn Residence, New York, New York, Khanna Cassabaum Design, interior designer; Seth Taras, photographer.

2, 3: Hiranandani Residence, Mumbai, India, TPA, architect; Ameya Gokaram, photographer.

4, 5: Private Residence, Gladwyne, Pennsylvania, Point B Design, aaaarchitect.

6: Cutler Residence, New York, New York, Poonam Khanna Cassabaum Design, interior designer; Seth Taras, photographer.

Bouyea & Associates, Inc.

5 Green Hill Road
P.O. Box 40
Washington Depot, CT 06794
860.868.4500
860.868.4501 (Fax)
www.bouyea.com

Bouyea & Associates, Inc.

Residences

Because every residence is unique, Bouyea & Associates works with clients, architects and interior designers to create distinctive environments that express the clients' personal values and preferences while showcasing the aesthetics of their homes. The firm's versatility can be seen in two recent examples: a new, 16,000-square-foot traditional home, designed by Richard Drummond Davis Architect and Lander Merchantile, and a remodeled, 3,000-square-foot contemporary home, designed by Allen Kirsch & Associates. Having previously occupied a 3,000-square-foot residence, the traditional client requested that the lighting simultaneously create a mood of warmth and intimacy within the new and larger space, and dramatize its outstanding architecture. The lighting design succeeds by highlighting objects within the rooms and incorporating low-voltage VNSP beams in the elaborate ceilings. The contemporary client wanted to maintain the architectural character of the home while accentuating a major art collection. The ceilings lacked sufficient depth for recessed lights, therefore low-voltage PAR lamps are used for precise beam control, warmth and lack of glare, and small, 4-inch quartz uplights provide ambient light, giving the space height and drawing attention to the architecture. For a home published in *House Beautiful* in 1963, its image glows even brighter today.

Bouyea & Associates, Inc.

Fairmont Scottsdale Princess
Willow Stream Spa
Scottsdale, Arizona

An oasis hidden deep in the Grand Canyon has provided inspiration for the Willow Stream Spa at Fairmont Scottsdale Princess, in Scottsdale, Arizona. This exceptional, 16,000-square-foot facility is designed by Three Architecture, architect, and Brayton Hughes Design Studio, interior designer. Based on the premise that a spa should awaken our senses, the goal for Bouyea & Associates as lighting designer has been to play up Willow Stream's indigenous materials and finishes and thereby enhance the ambience of nature evident throughout the space. Numerous lighting techniques are employed to achieve this, without ever having light fall directly on any guest. Grazing the stone and tile with light, for example, accents the tactile sense of these materials. In addition, the selection of beautiful color temperatures in the lights establishes a relaxing environment overall. The illumination of a cove with cold cathode accentuates the blue domed ceiling, and the installation of a PAR cove accents the texture of the back glass tile wall and brings out warmer tones. The result is a balanced composition of warm and cool tones, neatly paralleling the fire and water themes celebrated by Willow Stream Spa.

1: Fairmont Scottsdale Princess, Willow Stream Spa, Scottsdale, Arizona, Three Architecture, architect; Brayton Hughes Design Studio, interior designer; Michael Wilson, photographer.

Bouyea & Associates, Inc.

American Airlines Admirals Club
Dallas/Fort Worth International Airport
DFW Airport, Texas

American Airlines now projects a confident and inspiring corporate image in its Admirals Club at Dallas/Fort Worth International Airport. The recent renovation and expansion of this 30,000-square-foot flagship installation, featuring interior design by Harris Design Associates and award-winning lighting design by Bouyea & Associates, celebrates American's local origin as well as its stature as the world's largest scheduled passenger airline. Lighting plays a major role in the project. Overcoming American's concerns about the previous lighting scheme as it fulfills the interior designer's desire to accentuate interior finish materials and integrate lighting within the architecture, and the art consultant's request to display the art of 26 Texas artists. In the bar and lounge, for example, halogen PAR lamps outline the texture of split-face limestone, A-lamp downlights softly brighten lounge areas, halogen PAR downlights define the marble-paved circulation path, and cold cathode tubes backlight the glass-paneled ceiling over the bar. Dallas artist Frances Bagley's sculpture, "Bronze Vessels" features incandescent PAR lamps mounted inside a ceiling pocket to contrast its silhouettes against a stone wall. A computer-controlled dimming system reduces the actual lighting load 21 percent below designated levels for energy savings American and its customers can appreciate.

1, 2: American Airlines Admirals Club, Dallas/Fort Worth International Airport, DFW, Texas, Harris Design Associates, interior designer; Michael Wilson, photographer.

Bouyea & Associates, Inc.

Hospitality

Today's travelers expect distinctive experiences, and Bouyea & Associates designs lighting that develops the full potential in projects by leading hospitality architects and interior designers. In collaborating on the design of the Four Seasons Resort Hualalai at Hawaii's historic Ka'upulehu with Hill Glazier Architects and James Northcutt Associates Interiors, Bouyea illuminated the 40-acre beachfront resort and its 72 buildings to emphasize its island setting. Island lighting restrictions protecting the University of Hawaii's Mees Solar Observatory were met by turning each building into a lantern rather than lighting its exterior. Highlights include the pool, illuminated by PAR 56 lamps, and the lobby, where quartz and A-lamps brighten the chandelier and ceiling. At the Four Seasons Resort Whistler, Fifty-two 80 Bistro, in Whistler Blackcomb, British Columbia, Canada, Bouyea served as lighting designer with Burrow Huggins Architects and Brayton Hughes Design Studio to provide a sparkling, daytime framework for spectacular mountain views and a rich, warm ambience for evenings. In the 160-seat Bistro, lighting alters moods for every meal, uplights stone columns to emphasize texture, individually lights tables with low voltage PAR beams, and accents a fireplace with a PAR cove. The 2010 Winter Olympics in Whistler Blackcomb will find a ready welcome here.

1: **Four Seasons Resort Whistler,** Blackcomb, British Columbia, Canada, Burrow Huggins Architects, architect; Brayton Hughes Design Studio, interior designer; John Sutton, photographer.

2, 3, 4: **Four Seasons Resort Hualalai,** Ka'upulehu, Hawaii, Hill Glazier Architects, architect; James Northcutt Associates Interiors, interior designer; James Wilson, photographer.

Bouyea & Associates, Inc.

Ritz-Carlton Central Park South
New York, New York

Manhattan's former St. Moritz Hotel had a highly respectable character of its own, but the building's recent conversion into the Ritz-Carlton Central Park South has raised the standards considerably higher. Thus, the renovation of the public areas, involving interior design by Frank Nicholson and lighting design by Bouyea & Associates includes the lobby, lounges, corridors, restaurant and bar. Guests are offered a harmonious blend of monumental architectural grandeur with intimate charm to accompany their stay in one of the world's most vibrant cities. A close look at the lobby demonstrates how fabulous, intimate lighting can coexist with extremely high ceilings. Among the lighting techniques used in the long, narrow and high space are a concealed incandescent cove that illuminates the vaulted, gold-leafed ceiling, a decorative chandelier whose low-level lighting complements the ceiling, champagne gold downlights that create pools of light on the patterned marble floor, and picture lighting with special optics to display a museum-quality painting by American artist Samuel Halpert. The result should delight newcomers to Ritz-Carlton's accommodations and satisfy the most demanding devotees of this legendary hotel group.

1: **Ritz-Carlton Central Park South,** New York, New York, Frank Nicholson, interior designer; Michael Wilson, photographer.

Brilliant Lighting Design

750 NE 61Street
Suite #201
Miami, FL 33137
305.751.7200
305.751.7200 (Fax)
www.brilliantlightingdesign.com

Brilliant Lighting Design

High-Rise Office Exteriors

How can a high-rise office tower stand out against a city's skyline at night? The answer is great lighting design. Lighting a tall building takes precise engineering and understanding of beam control. Since partially lighting the top alone seldom looks good, Robert Daniels of Brilliant Lighting Design takes the time to define the building's shape aesthetically and achieve a complete look. Difficult as it is to throw light long distances, the firm has succeeded in single throws of light to 220 meters and filtered light to 190 meters, and hopes to illuminate a 350-meter tower someday. A properly lighted tall building sends a dramatic message that can be read over surprisingly long distances. Not only will the building be seen from close by, its crown or top will be visible for up to two miles away, a feat successfully accomplished by Brilliant Lighting Design for many clients.

1: **Torre Global,** Panama City, Rep. of Panama, Pinzon Lozano & Assoc. Architects; IESNA Nat'l "Award of Merit"

2: **Banco Popular Center,** San Juan, Puerto Rico, Kahn & Jacobs, Toro & Ferrer, architects.

3: **2100 Ponce de Leon,** Coral Gables, Florida.

4, 5: **Colpatria Tower,** Bogota, Colombia, Oscar Jaime Obando, architect, IESNA Paul Waterbury Int'l "Award of Excellence"

1

2

3

4

5

Brilliant Lighting Design

Classic Buildings and Churches

Few sights are as stirring to residents and visitors of great cities during the evening hours than the lighting of their classic buildings and churches. The illumination of these edifices is a particular joy and professional challenge to the lighting designer. For Robert Daniels of Brilliant Lighting Design, classic buildings provide an opportunity to make light work in unusual ways. The successful lighting design begins with creative planning to cover the myriad of detailed surfaces. As a result, the classic building assumes different personalities by day and night. In the daytime, the building's details are uniformly displayed with light coming from above. By contrast, selective night lighting can emphasize the best tympanums, friezes, and other details through brightness, angles and colors. The contrasting portrayal can be provocative enough to encourage people to revisit the classic building they know by day to witness its transformation in the hours of the night—by lighting.

1: **Bascillica Don Bosco,** Panama City, Panama.

2: **Georgia State Capitol,** Atlanta, Georgia, IESNA Nat'l "Award of Merit"

3, 4: **National Sanctuary Church,** Panama City, Panama, GE Edison Int'l "Award of Excellence"

Brilliant Lighting Design

Bridges

That bridges, highways or other creations by civil engineers can rise to the level of art becomes apparent to anyone experiencing them by day. At night, their imagery can become magical. To show the client's bridge to best advantage, Robert Daniels of Brilliant Lighting Design begins planning the lighting design by considering four viewing areas: the angled view from above, the perpendicular view from boats in the water, the view under the bridge adjacent to the abutment, and the view of the traveler over the top of the bridge. In addition to highlighting the bridge itself, the design must fit the bridge into the city skyline. Ethereal as the outcome may appear, it should also be preceded by numerous mundane considerations, such as fixture positioning, a restrictive exercise compounded by anti-vandalism measures, as well as the need for anti-corrosion materials and easy maintenance procedures. But the precautions are justified the moment the lights come on.

1: **Bridge of the Americas,** Canal Zone, Rep. of Panama, IESNA Nat'l "Award of Merit"; GE Edison Int'l "Award of Merit"; *Architectural Lighting Magazine* 2005 Design Awards "Best Project on a Budget"

2: **MacArthur Causeway Bridge,** Miami, Florida, GE Edison Int'l "Award of Excellence"; IESNA Nat'l "Award of Merit"

3: **Lane Avenue Bridge,** Columbus, Ohio, IESNA Nat'l "Award of Merit"

Brilliant Lighting Design

Casino and Lounge Interiors

Nothing is simple about the light that supports the stagecraft of casino and lounge interiors, and the effective lighting design requires innovative use of new and existing light sources. At the same time light amazes the guest through contrast and variations, it must enhance the interior designer's environment by creating the appropriate mood and theme in areas large and small. The expertise of Robert Daniels of Brilliant Lighting Design is demonstrated at the Jester Lounge, in Panama City, Florida, by the variegated lighted ceiling, Erte window wall light box, and glowing alabaster U-shaped bar. Elegance permeates the Crown Casino, also in Panama City, thanks to the golden theme at the entrance and the color-changing waves of LED light moving along the full length of the main gaming room to relax guests for longer periods of play. Whatever goals set by the interior design for the casino or lounge, the lighting will be part of the action.

1: **Jester Lounge,** Panama City, Rep. of Panama, Mallol & Mallol Architects

2, 3: **Crown Casino Continental Riande Hotel,** Panama City, Rep. of Panama, IESNA Nat'l "Award of Merit"

Brilliant Lighting Design

Hotel and Condominium Exteriors

Walk, drive or fly past a hotel or condominium at night, and it's easy to see why a dramatically lighted façade would tempt you to register more readily than an unlighted one. Savvy hotels and condominiums do indeed gain public recognition and enhance reputation through the images they project after nightfall. However, developing lighting to enhance the unusual shapes of these buildings requires a high level of artistic and architectural understanding. The work of Robert Daniels of Brilliant Lighting Design in illuminating hotel and condominium exteriors deliberately places creative emphasis on their structural features—at the same time light intrusion is reduced to a minimum. As a precaution to building owners, it should be noted that engineering the lighting with appropriate glare control is a must to satisfy occupants. The goal is to create a lighted oasis for the surrounding neighborhood, an oasis that attracts customers every time the sun goes down.

1, 3: Golden Moon Hotel & Casino, Philadelphia, Mississippi, Arquitectonica, architects.
2002 GE Edison Award winner (top lighting design in the world).
2003 IESNA Paul Waterbury Int'l "Award of Excellence."
2003 IALD Int'l "Award of Merit."

2: Vue Condominium, Miami, Florida, Bermillo, Ajamil & Partners Architect; IESNA Nat'l "Award of Merit."

4: Sheraton Biscayne Bay, Miami, Florida.

5: Villa Regina Condominium, Miami, Florida, Yakov Agam, architect.

Brilliant Lighting Design

Landscape and Fountains

As every architect or landscape architect knows, trees and other elements of landscape represent an ideal accompaniment for buildings. For lighting designers, the relationship of trees to man-made structures presents unique opportunities to create special illumination at night. Designing a lighted environment of landscape and hardscape is extremely difficult. For example, trees and other plants vary in their size, shape, texture and color, and the range of specimens must be considered in the design. Robert Daniels of Brilliant Lighting Design works to develop unfolding vistas from both exterior and interior settings to produce distinctive, lighted scenes. Being sensitive to the dynamics of the garden, Brilliant Lighting Design takes care to find plants that will serve as the best-lighted specimens within the framework of the overall scene.

1: **Centro Sambil Galleria Cascades,** Caracas, Venezuela.

2, 3: **Burek Residence,** Coconut Grove, Florida.

4: **Eiber Residence,** Miami Beach, Florida.

Brilliant Lighting Design

Interiors/Art Galleries

Can you imagine a successful art gallery, hair salon, or restaurant without its lighting design? Impossible, you say? That's because the lighting of the most effective commercial interiors closely follows the theme of the architect or interior designer and the highlights of individual rooms. Thus, an art gallery focuses on the artworks, a hair salon highlights the cutting surface, a condominium lobby facilitates casual waiting and conversation, and a restaurant concentrates on the ambience at each table as well as buffet areas. On the other hand, Robert Daniels of Brilliant Lighting Design realizes that good commercial illumination must also look beyond areas where tasks are performed to highlight walls or other features, being sure to integrate them with the service function of the space. Though patrons of popular restaurants don't consume the ambience of a well-illuminated interior, they would sense an immediate diminishing of the dining experience without it.

1: **Vue Condominium,** Miami, Florida, Bermello, Ajamil & Partners, Architect, IESNA Nat'l "Award of Merit".

2: **Midori Galleries,** Coconut Grove, Florida.

3: **Lyons Hair Salon,** South Miami, Florida.

CD+M Lighting Design Group

ATLANTA
655 Highland Avenue #3
Atlanta, GA 30312
404.522.9911
404.522.915 (Fax)

LOS ANGELES
15549 Devonshire Street
Ste. 4
Mission Hills, CA 91345
818.830.2323
818.830.2324 (Fax)

www.cdmlight.com

ORLANDO
770 W. Bay St
Winter Garden, FL 34787
407.656.9996
678.904.5360 (Fax)

CHINA
29/F Unit D, Building A
INNOTEC Tower
No.235 Nanjing Road, Heping
District
Tianjin 300052, CHINA
022.2721.7115
022.2721.7117 (Fax)

CD+M Lighting Design Group
Museum and Exhibit Lighting

With numerous museum projects to its credit—such as the COSI Children's Museum in Columbus, OH, the Mayo Clinic Heritage Hall in Rochester, MN, and the Texas State History Museum in Austin, TX —CD+M Lighting Design has developed a successful approach to museum lighting emphasizing that lighting equipment should be nearly invisible to guests. Good lighting draws focus to the exhibits, increasing the contrast in light levels between focal areas and background surfaces to create dramatic effects. However, lighting equipment must blend with architecture, multimedia systems and exhibitry to avoid

attracting attention to itself. Among the resources CD+M Lighting Design prefers for museum and exhibit lighting are low voltage halogen lamps and small PAR lamps, offering compact size, excellent color rendering and abundant fixtures designed for them, and highly adjustable lighting fixtures that allow the use of light control devices such as shutters, lenses and glare hoods, preventing direct view of light sources and shaping beams of light as required. The result: exciting museum spaces and exhibits guests want to experience.

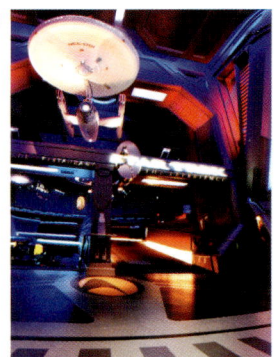

1, 7: Spacepark, Bremen, Germany, Rhode Kellerman Wawrowsky, architect; Landmark Entertainment Group, attraction design; Ted Ferreira, lighting design (concept); Durham Marenghi, lighting design (production); Spacepark Betriebs GmbH, photography.

2: Volkswagen Glaserne Manufactur, Dresden, Germany, BRC Imagination Arts, exhibit design; CD+M Lighting Design, lighting design (exhibit); Kardoff Ingenieure, lighting design (facility); BRC Imagination Arts, photography.

3: Star Trek—The Experience, Las Vegas, NV, Landmark Entertainment Group, attraction design; CD+M Lighting Design, lighting design; Gary Zee Opulence Studios, photography.

4: Ngong Ping 360, Hong Kong, Dedica Group: Creative Design and Management, attraction producer; CD+M Lighting Design, lighting design; Dedica Group, photography.

5: Georgia Aquarium, Atlanta, GA, Thompson Ventulett Stainback & Associates, architect; Peckham Guyton Albers & Viets, exhibit designer; Heery International, program manager; Gary Goddard Entertainment, attraction design; CD+M Lighting Design, lighting design (4-D theatre, lantern wall, Plaza, specialty lighting); Kieran Reynolds, photography.

6: Ford Rouge Visitors Center, Dearborn, Michigan, William McDonough & Partners, architect; BRC Imagination Arts, exhibit design; CD+ M Lighting Design, lighting design.

CD+M Lighting Design Group
Leisure and Gaming Lighting

Does the guest crave elaborate fantasy or simple elegance? Themes typically inspire leisure and gaming facilities, and CD+M Lighting Design creates lighting environments to reinforce and enhance themes developed by architects and interior designers for projects as varied as SeaWorld, Orlando, Showcentre Norte, Buenos Aires, Argentina, and Mandalay Bay Hotel & Casino, Las Vegas. Lighting for leisure and gaming requires a focused approach to attract guests to the most prominent features of a project, using color, movement and theatrical techniques to add excitement and variety. Large projects must be considered in terms of their components. Within gaming areas, overall ambient light levels should be reduced as much as possible to make such key areas as gaming pits focal points on the casino floor. CD+M Lighting Design uses incandescent lamps wherever practical, typically low voltage adjustable luminaires for their compact size, warmth and ability to be completely dimmed, ideal qualities for creating inviting settings. Color abounds in gaming, but white light is required for gaming table surveillance and monitoring.

1

2

3

4

1: **SeaWorld Mistify Summer Spectacular,** Orlando, FL, 5 Star Entertainment, attraction producer; CD+M Lighting Design, lighting design; Kevin Kolczynski, photography.

2: **Universal Islands of Adventure,** Orlando, FL, Poseidon's Adventure Attraction, Gary Goddard Entertainment, attraction design; Ted Ferreira, lighting design (re-design); Kevin Kolczynski, photography.

3: **Mandalay Bay Hotel & Casino,** Las Vegas, NV, Klai + Juba Architects, architect; Dougall Design Associates, interior design; Marc Rosenberg for Marcad Lighting Design, lighting design.

4: **Universal Islands of Adventure,** Orlando, FL, Jurassic Park: Ted Ferreira for Universal Studios Planning and Development and Passamonte Lighting Design, lighting designers (park specifications, site lighting, controls design), Universal Studios Florida, photography.

5: **Caesar's Palace Forum Shops,** Las Vegas, NV, Kittrell Garlock and Associates, architect; Dougall Design Associates, interior design; Shawn Whitaker for Marcad Lighting Design, lighting designer, Dougall Design Associates, photography.

CD+M Lighting Design Group

Hospitality and Convention Center Lighting

A warm, inviting atmosphere where people feel relaxed and comfortable is vital to hospitality lighting, and our designers have worked with architects and interior designers to achieve this in such major projects as THEhotel at Mandalay Bay, Las Vegas, Mandarin Oriental Hotel, New York, and Four Seasons' Gresham Palace, Budapest, Hungary. Hospitality and convention projects often employ multiple layers of lighting that create visual interest and promote wayfinding in key areas while simultaneously establishing a pleasing overall ambiance. A large decorative fixture can set the mood in a lobby, giving guests their first impression. Elsewhere, corridor lighting should make room numbers and keys legible and shorten perceived distances, table and floor lamps in guests rooms impart a residential feel, and ballroom lighting operates at three levels: immense decorative fixtures for centerpieces, halogen downlights for detail and cove lighting, and/or wall sconces for dimension and height. CD+M Lighting Design prefers incandescent and halogen lamps in hospitality for their emphasis on reds and yellows and their dimming capabilities, teamed with such decorative light fixtures as chandeliers, table lamps, floor lamps and picture lights. Ironically, though daylight is too unpredictable for most hospitality projects, convention centers prize it for reducing electricity demand during daytime hours.

1: Mandarin Oriental Hotel, New York, NY, Brennan Beer Gorman, architect; Hirsch Bedner Associates, interior design; Hilary Wainer for PHA, lighting design.

2: Rio Hotel and Convention Center, Las Vegas, NV, Marnell Corrao Associates, architect; Marc Rosenberg, lighting design, Marnell Corrao Associates, photography.

3: Inn of the Mountain Gods, Mescalero, NM, WorthGroup, architect and interior design; Marc Rosenberg, lighting design; John Wong, photography.

4: Mandarin Oriental Hotel, Miami, FL, RTKL, architect; Hirsch Bedner Associates, interior design; Hilary Wainer for PHA, lighting design.

5: THEhotel at Mandalay Bay, Las Vegas, NV, Klai + Juba, architect; Dougall Design Associates, interior design; Marc Rosenberg, lighting design; Dennis Anderson, photography.

CD+M Lighting Design Group

Education Lighting

Lighting's role in education is critical, as CD+M Lighting Design has maintained in contributing for such notable clients as Case Western Reserve University, University of Georgia, Emory University, Auburn University, the University of North Carolina, and other institutions. Good lighting provided by energy efficient, low brightness luminaries can maximize learning potential at the same time it reduces distractions caused by inadequate light levels, glare and reflections. Classroom lighting should generally exhibit medium intensity and uniformity, with such important areas as blackboards or whiteboards receiving high levels to reduce eye strain and eliminate shadowing. Computer laboratories require special attention, since educators must be able to increase contrast

1, 4: Case Western University, Weatherhead Graduate School of Management, Cleveland, OH, Frank O. Gehry, architect; CD+M, Lighting Design; Lucci & Associates, specialty electrical engineering.

2, 3: University of Georgia, East Campus Dining Facility, Athens, GA, Collins, Cooper, Carusi, architect; CD+M Lighting Design, lighting design, Creative Sources Photography.

between ambient light and the screen for greater legibility in these facilities by reducing light levels. CD+M Lighting Design prefers fluorescent lamps in a mix of 1x4 or 2x4 fixtures and direct/indirect linear fixtures for long life, energy efficiency, cost effectiveness, omni-directional capability, glare control and precise optics. Also worth noting is the trend toward LEED-certified school construction, which is bringing more daylight into buildings. Daylighting requires intricate control systems to implement properly, but reduces demand for electric light and conserves energy. Not surprisingly, many educational facilities are now models of green building.

C.M. Kling & Associates, Inc.

1411 King Street
Alexandria, VA 22314
703.684.6270
703.684.6273 (Fax)
www.cmkling.com
light@cmkling.com

C.M. Kling & Associates, Inc.

Knoxville Convention Center
Knoxville, Tennessee

1 - 3: Knoxville Convention Center, Knoxville, Tennessee, Thompson, Ventulett, Stainback & Associates, and McCarty, Holsaple, McCarty, architects; Brian Gassel/TVS (1) Robert Batey (2), photographers.

What does a community do for Act II after a World's Fair leaves town? For the City of Knoxville, Tennessee, the revitalization of World's Fair Park has begun auspiciously with the opening of the new, 500,000-square-foot Knoxville Convention Center, designed by the architecture firms Thompson, Ventulett, Stainback & Associates and McCarty, Holsaple, McCarty with C.M. Kling & Associates as lighting designer. Despite its monumental size and form, the Convention Center has been conceived as an inviting environment, deliberately echoing the shape of a Tennessee barn while offering an exhibit hall, meeting rooms, auditorium, public circulation spaces, prefunction and registration halls and a 27,000-square-foot ballroom. The award-winning lighting design enhances the vast glazed spaces by day and opens up the interior to public view at night, highlighting the silhouette of the building and making the glazed atrium transparent adding vitality to its surroundings. If the Convention Center is a harbinger of things to come, the future looks quite bright for the citizens of Knoxville.

C.M. Kling & Associates, Inc.

Woolly Mammoth Theatre
Washington, D.C.

Traditional as the cultural life of the nation's capital generally is, theater audiences have a strong appetite for a wide range of productions, setting the stage for the new, 265-seat Woolly Mammoth Theatre. This first-time home of the leading-edge production company founded in 1980, designed by McInturff Architects with C.M. Kling & Associates as lighting designer, could be best described as raw design on a shoestring budget. Yet, despite the predominance of concrete and cinderblock construction, there is room for artistry in such elements as the central ceiling plane, traversing the length of the lobby, and the three-story, curved and translucent wall. The lighting design honors the spirit of the architecture by eschewing recessed lighting in favor of fully exposed, utilitarian fixtures, which function quite suitably for such public spaces as the lobby, gathering area, ticket office, retail shop, café and circulation house, as well as the stage and backstage facilities. The fixtures can transform the space with the aid of color filters that are easily accessed from the front of the panels, a reminder that the award-winning lighting design complements the theater because both support the idea that day after day, the show must go on.

1 - 3: Woolly Mammoth Theatre, auditorium, Washington, D.C., McInturff Architects, architect; Julian Heine, photographer.

C.M. Kling & Associates, Inc.

Charlotte Douglas International Airport
West Daily Parking Deck
Charlotte, North Carolina

Drivers instantly recognize that the new West Daily Parking Deck at Charlotte Douglas International Airport, in Charlotte, North Carolina, exceeds the boundaries of conventional parking garage design. How could they not? The new, five-level, one million-square-foot structure, designed by Wilson Group and LS3P Associates as architects with C.M. Kling & Associates as lighting designer, provides what too many of these facilities cannot deliver. It establishes an attractive, safe and secure environment even for people who are not in their cars. The tightly choreographed relationship between architecture and lighting helps explain the award-winning achievement. For example, perforated metal panels, backlighted blue, match the airport's accent color and offer visibility to meet airport safety requirements while revealing the trusses behind them. Concrete columns, grazed with white light, contrast with the panels. Circular penetrations in entry/exit helix barrier walls are fitted with blue LED signal lights programmed to chase around the helix, mimicking the path of a driver and adding a dynamic element to the design. Other examples of lighting defining space can be found throughout the parking decks, elevator lobbies and stairwells. Most parking garages are "background buildings," but the West Daily Parking Deck should be seen in a whole new light.

1 - 3: Charlotte Douglas International Airport, West Daily Parking Deck, Charlotte, North Carolina, Wilson Group, LS3P Associates, architects; Carolina Photo Group, photographer.

C.M. Kling & Associates, Inc.

Public Spaces

No one questions the use of lighting in monumental public buildings and spaces to enhance the stature of the architecture. But can lighting play a part in the sustainability of these facilities as well? In its role as lighting designer for public buildings, including those depicted here, C.M. Kling & Associates pays close attention to the concept of sustainability for maintenance of the overall design as well as environmental impact. Furthermore, a public structure should be considered for its internal surfaces as well as exterior façade, and one with extensive curtainwall glazing may be more interesting with its interior illuminated, making the glass transparent. How are public spaces lighted? Basic components include such lamps as LED, incandescent halogen, metal halide and fluorescent, and such luminaires as uplights, bollards, poles, recessed downlights and wall washers. Color can have an exciting impact too, as uplighting with a purple gel shows at The Baltimore Visitors Center, promoting the local NFL team and coinciding with similar purple lighting elsewhere in the city. It goes without saying that low wattage, high efficiency lamps and efficient fixtures must be used wherever possible for energy conservation, a measure both public and private sectors can unequivocally endorse.

1: **The Baltimore Visitors Center,** Baltimore, Maryland, Design Collective Inc., architect; DCG, photographer.

2: **Gulf State Park Beach Pavilion,** Gulf Shores, Alabama, Thompson, Ventulett, Stainback & Associates, architect; Peter Green, photographer.

3, 4: **Washington, D.C. Convention Center,** Washington, D.C., Thompson, Ventulett, Stainback & Associates, architect; Brian Gassel/TVS, photographer.

C.M. Kling & Associates, Inc.

Hospitality

Have you attended banquets where speakers were nearly invisible? Knowing how complex lighting for hospitality can be, C.M. Kling & Associates focuses on three layers: of light general, flexible illumination, sparkle and accent lighting. Too often hotel lighting is designed for a specific visual image with little regard to the activities it serves. Ballrooms, for example, require flexible lighting for multiple functions to simultaneously provide even illumination and key accent lighting for head tables. Restaurants typically deviate from designers' seating plans, favoring flexible designs using general ambient light layered with sparkle for art, millwork or display kitchens over schemes that highlight individual table tops. Exterior lighting should increase a project's visibility without trespassing into guest rooms. To light hospitality facilities, the firm uses such lamps as halogen, LED, limited dimmable fluorescent, and energy saving compact fluorescent and metal halide, and such luminaires as low-voltage track, recessed downlights, wall washers, accent lights, chandeliers and sconces. And the job's not done without examining the color of lighting. Fun and visually fascinating as colored lighting can be, the lighting of a hospitality facility should primarily enhance colors and textures selected by the architect and/or interior designer, and minimize color's potential conflict with the tasks at hand.

1: Marriott World Center Orlando, Orlando, Florida, Thompson, Ventulett, Stainback & Associates, architect.

2: Waldorf-Astoria, Peacock Alley, New York, New York, Arnold Syrop Associates, architect, Edward Jacoby, photographer.

3: Waldorf-Astoria, New York, New York, Kenneth E. Hurd & Associates, interior designer; photography courtesy of Waldorf-Astoria.

4: Hilton Boston Logan Airport, Boston, Massachusetts, Cambridge Seven Associates, architect; Peter Vanderwarker, © vanderwarker.com, photographer.

C.M. Kling & Associates, Inc.

Corporate

Lighting corporate spaces may be more complicated than business people appreciate, providing an environment that positively displays corporate identity while encouraging employee productivity. In serving the corporate world, C.M. Kling & Associates deals with lighting's total impact on the environment, involving interior design as well as exterior architecture, so that light placement and lamp selection can realize the potential drama and spatial depth envisioned by the architect or interior designer using high-end materials and finishes. Lighting can make a difference in such locations as the façade, canopy and entry drive, where it introduces the corporate image, the lobby or atrium, where it welcomes employees and visitors, and the reception desk, private offices, general office space, and boardroom, where it "brands" space and supports activity. Such lamps as LED, incandescent fluorescent, metal halide, and fluorescent, and luminaires ranging from decorative pendants and sconces to recessed downlighting and accent lights, enable the lighting design to match the architectural style of the space. Beyond style, the lighting design of today's corporate space must also include low-wattage, high-efficiency lamps, efficient fixtures, and state-of-the-art controls to reduce overall energy use and extend lamp life in everything from the humblest branch office to the grandest headquarters.

1: **One Ten Lincoln Street,** Boston, Massachusetts, Jung Brannen Associates, architect; Peter Vanderwarker, © vanderwarker.com, photographer.

2: **Institute of International Economics,** Washington, D.C., Kohn Pedersen Fox Architects, architect; Michael Dersin, photographer.

3, 4: **Medimmune,** Gaithersburg, Maryland, Hellmuth, Obata & Kassabaum, architect; Ron Solomon, photographer.

C.M. Kling & Associates, Inc.

Houses of Worship

If light is a powerful symbol in spirituality, it is equally potent as a sculptor of places of worship. C.M. Kling & Associates, Inc. combines multiple lighting approaches to support tasks and create moods in facilities as monumental as the Washington National Cathedral, in Washington, D.C., and as intimate as a neighborhood church. Pews need even illumination, for example, so prayer books can be comfortably read. The stage requires much higher levels of light, properly angled to define the speaker's face without harshness. Architectural details and liturgical furnishings have to be properly lighted to create the atmosphere that the congregation wishes to convey. Of course, the equipment must be technically and aesthetically appropriate. Since halogen dims easily, has excellent color rendering, creates sparkle and drama, and handles tall ceilings, it is commonly used. Fixtures generally reflect the architecture and desired image of the space therefore, opulent decorative pieces grace ornate interiors, and track lighting highlights liturgical furnishings and the stage in modern settings. Lighting controls also play an important role, responding to changing activities and the time of day by creating different looks or scenes, raising lighting levels at night, and achieving special effects for holidays and other special events.

1: **Washington National Cathedral,** Washington, D.C., photograph courtesy of Washington National Cathedral.

2: **Holy Trinity Catholic Church,** Washington, D.C., Kerns Group Architects, architect; Michael Dersin, photographer.

3: **St. Mary's Episcopal Church,** Vienna, Virginia, Kerns Group Architects, architect; Michael Dersin, photographer.

Domingo Gonzalez Associates

25 Park Place
5th Floor
New York, NY 10007
212.608.4800
212.385.9160 (Fax)
www.dgalight.com

Domingo Gonzalez Associates

Corporate/Institutional

For corporations and institutions, workplace lighting frequently reveals their identities as well as their activities. Serving numerous corporate and institutional clients, DGA knows how demanding their requirements can be. At the New-York Historical Society, in New York's Upper West Side, the firm assisted in the restoration and upgrade of the historic 1904 landmark structure originally designed by architect York & Sawyer, installing energy-conscious, artwork-sensitive, historically responsive lighting systems for such facilities as the first-floor galleries, lower-level multi-purpose areas, seminar rooms, library (below), entries and exterior façade. For the conference center at 485 Lexington Avenue,

the new TIAA-CREF Building in midtown Manhattan, the firm illuminated such spaces as the subdividable meeting and conference rooms, lobbies and pre-function areas as well as the main lobby, where compact metal halide lighting makes the onyx paneled feature wall glow. In the 1904 landmark Neo-Gothic building, Shepard Hall, originally designed by architect George B. Post for the City College of New York, the firm's lighting design involved the redesign, replication and refurbishment of historic chandeliers, downlights, sconces and pendants along with the introduction of supplemental architectural and theatrical lighting.

1

1: **New-York Historical Society,** Beyer Blinder Belle, architect; John Bartelstone, photographer. 2000 Lucy B. Moses Preservation Design Award and 2001 New York State AIA Award.

2: **485 Lexington Avenue,** Conference Center and Lobby, New York, New York, KPF, architect; John Bartelstone, photographer.

3: **New York State Apellate Court,** Albany, NY, Ricci Greene, architect; Byorg Maega, photographer. 2006 IIDA/IES Award of Merit.

4, 5: **City College of New York,** Shepard Hall, New York, New York, Stein White, architect; John Bartelstone, photographer. 1998 Lucy B. Moses Preservation Design Award.

Domingo Gonzalez Associates

Retailing/Museums/Exhibitions

How to illuminate an entire space yet focus attention on selected areas is the problem facing lighting designers working with architects and interior designers in retailing, museums and exhibitions. Effective solutions as developed by DGA, require appropriate lamp selection to establish ambient lighting as a context for more dramatic focused lighting, as well as luminaires that range from concealed, built-in fixtures to decorative fixtures that function as prominent design elements. This approach can be seen in the café, book store and gift shops that the firm illuminated at the New York Botanical Garden's new 27,500-square-foot visitors center in The Bronx, along with the building's offices, restrooms, exterior entry pylons and walkways. Striking a satisfying balance between overall space and specific displays presented a similar challenge for the firm in the new Henry Luce III Center for the Study of American Culture, where an entire collection of artifacts in various shapes and sizes is shown at all times, and in other display areas at Manhattan's New-York Historical Society, the object of a lengthy restoration and upgrade of its historic 1904 home.

1, 2: **New York Botanical Garden,** Visitors Center, The Bronx, New York, HHPA, architect; John Bartelstone, photographer. New York Construction 2004 Cultural Award of Merit, 2004 GE Edison Lighting Award of Merit.

3: **St. John the Divine Cathedral,** Glass Sculpture Display, New York, New York, John Bartelstone, photographer.

4, 5: **New-York Historical Society,** , Henry Luce III Center for the Study of American Culture, Free Press exhibition, New York, New York, Beyer Blinder Belle, architect; John Bartelstone, photographer. 2000 Lucy B. Moses Preservation Design Award, 2001 New York State AIA Award.

Domingo Gonzalez Associates

Transportation

Vast and complex as many transportation facilities are, their lighting must facilitate wayfinding so travelers can find their destinations quickly and easily. Lighting works in concert with architecture, signage, sound and other navigational systems to guide travelers, reveal form, and celebrate civic identity. The results can be both practical and beautiful. DGA's work on the new World Trade Center transportation hub in lower Manhattan, featuring a headhouse (below right) designed by Santiago Calatrava, offers lighting solutions to complement the architecture and direct millions of commuters on their way. At JFK International Airport's new light rail system, which links JFK to the New York City subway system, the firm has created exterior and interior lighting systems for the platforms, connectors, lobbies, transfer nodes and exterior canopies of nine light rail stations. Another critical transit connection is illuminated by the firm's design for the new, three-level, 600,000-square-foot station in New Jersey's Hackensack Meadowlands, marking the intersection of the New Jersey Transit mainline and Amtrak's Northeast Corridor and making platforms, stairs, waiting areas, mezzanines, station concourse and retail areas easy to find and use.

1, 7: JFK International Airport, Light Rail System, Queens, New York, STV, architect; John Bartelstone, photographer. 2002 New York Construction Airport Project of the Year Award, 2004 New York Construction Award of Merit.

2: Secaucus Junction, Secaucus, New Jersey, BBG, architect; John Bartelstone, photographer. 2003 New York Construction Transit Project of the Year Award.

3: World Trade Center Temporary PATH Station, New York, New York, Port Authority of New York and New Jersey, architect; John Bartelstone, photographer. 2004 New York Construction Transit Project of the Year Award, 2004 AIA Public Project of the Year Award.

4: Intermodal Ferry Terminal, New York, New York, WNBA, architect; John Bartelstone, photographer. 2005 GE Edison Lighting Award of Excellence, New York Construction 2005 Best Marine Project of the Year.

5: Hertz Rental Agency, Orlando, Florida, Richard Dattner Architects, architect; Richard Dattner, photographer.

6: World Trade Center Transportation Hub, New York, New York, Santiago Calatrava, architect; Illustration: Courtesy of Domingo Gonzalez Associates.

8: JFK International Airport, Terminal One, Queens, New York, WNBA, architect; John Bartelstone, photographer. 1998 New York Construction Airport Project of the Year Award.

4

7

5

8

6

Domingo Gonzalez Associates

Communities become safer, more manageable and inviting at night when bridges, streets and outdoor spaces are illuminated. DGA's work brings the night landscape to life. For example, the firm's work on New York's historic Washington Square Arch, part of a total restoration of the 1895 McKim, Mead and White monument, uses pole and grade-mounted metal halide sources and continuous, cornice-mounted T5HO fluorescent sources to create a brilliant terminus to Fifth Avenue. Along the first completed portion of New York's Hudson River Park, the firm developed design solutions, contract documents, calculations and specifications for the esplanade, piers, community gardens and elsewhere, helping return the waterfront to public use. In Nashville, drivers and pedestrians traveling between the historic downtown and new football stadium can see the magnificent result of the firm's lighting for the 1908 Shelby Street Bridge, including the approach ramps, outlooks, walkways, superstructure and support pylons. Equally important is the firm's comprehensive exterior flood-lighting strategy for lighting New York's George Washington Bridge towers, which produced a striking solution for the Port Authority of New York and New Jersey in time for the city's July 4, 2000 celebrations.

1: Washington Square Arch, New York, New York, John Bartelstone, photographer. 2003 Lucy B. Moses Preservation Award, 2004 New York Construction Award of Merit, GE /Edison Lighting Award of Excellence.

2: Hudson River Park, New York, New York, John Bartelstone, photographer. 2003 GE Edison Lighting Award of Merit, 2003 New York Construction Site & Planning Project of the Year.

3: Shelby Street Bridge, Nashville, Tennessee, Dave Anderson, photographer. 2003 ABC Award of Excellence, 2004 Excellence in Development Award, 2005 IIDA/IES Award of Merit.

4: George Washington Bridge, New York, New York, John Bartelstone, photographer. 2000 IES Lumen Award, 2001 GE Award of Excellence.

Fox & Fox Design

134 Main Street
Suite A
Seal Beach, CA 90740
562.799.8488
801.705.1290 (Fax)
www.foxandfoxdesign.com

Fox & Fox Design

High Moon Studios
Carlsbad, California

Why would anyone convert a spacious warehouse flooded by daylight from 30 skylights into a relatively dark, residential living room-style setting for a headquarters? The new, two-story, 120,000-square-foot studio and office of High Moon Studios, the video game publisher of "Darkwatch" and other popular titles, enables each of 100 game developers to operate effectively within a workstation equipped with four to six screens, thanks to a design by McLarand Vasquez Emsiek & Partners, architect, and Fox & Fox Design, lighting designer. The primary goal in developing the state-of-the-art facility for High Moon Studios (formerly Sammy Studios) has been to place the creative staff in "neighborhoods"—each resembling a different "world" depicted in video games—within an open environment dotted with such "structures" as a half pipe, rock climbing mountains, life guard towers and industrial buildings. To create optimum lighting, the design introduces "light columns" that harvest daylight from 10 of the 30 skylights, reducing the lighting level from 250 footcandles to about 14 footcandles. Two CFL highbays installed in each light column extend "daylight" beyond daytime with electric lighting, and they are supplemented by CFL swing-arm desk lamps. Consequently, developers enjoy high visibility for their screens—plus daylight without glare.

1 - 5: **High Moon Studios**, Carlsbad, California, McLarand Vasquez Emsiek & Partners, Inc., architect; Robert Hansen, photographer. 2004 IIDA Award, San Diego Section.

Fox & Fox Design

Shade Hotel
Manhattan Beach, California

Habitués of the legendary beach volleyball and surfing scene in California's Manhattan Beach might wonder about the new, chic nightspots just steps from the pier. However, when the two-story, 30,000-square-foot, 38-room Shade Hotel, designed by Tolkin & Associates, architect, Drasin Design, interior designer, Christopher Lowell, executive design director, and Fox & Fox Design, lighting designer, recently opened as Manhattan Beach's first luxury boutique hotel, a stylish crowd filled its lobby, Zinc Lounge, outdoor dining deck, guest suites, inner courtyard, pool and rooftop skydeck from day one. The Shade achieves its "yacht chic" look at a modest cost through artistry and resourcefulness. The outdoor dining deck's custom designed chandeliers, for example,

were outsourced from China, much as other FF&E items were. Elsewhere, the lighting is equally imaginative. Blue LED lighting is used thematically to portray the hotel as a "cool" retreat and to contrast with the warm and inviting interiors. Every guest suite incorporates a lighting control system that guest or front desk can operate to set a desired mood. Last but not least, the shoji-screened bath enclosure's chromatherapy lighting system lets the guest match the color to the moment—so hot it's cool for Manhattan Beach.

1 - 6: **Shade Hotel,** Manhattan Beach, California, Tolkin & Associates, architect; Drasin Design, interior designer; Christopher Lowell Show, executive design director; Jeffrie Bacic, John Fox, photographers.

Fox & Fox Design

Hospitality/Restaurant

If you've ever sensed you were on stage in a visit to a restaurant, hotel or other hospitality venue, you're not alone. Hospitality lighting is about theater. Lighting must shape the guest's experience so he or she feels enchanted, from the reservation confirmation by the host or front desk to the tip of the valet. The need to achieve and control the "layers" of light people experience for a few hours of time in all hospitality projects but especially in restaurants is well known to Fox & Fox Design, which serves well known establishments, such as Ruth's Chris Steak House, a worldwide chain, and individual restaurants, such as Petro's, in Manhattan Beach, California. To create the appropriate lighting

environment, the firm uses dimmable sources that can adjust the mood for the time of day, drawing heavily on incandescent and/or low-voltage white light as well as CFL for maximal color rendition, along with HID and LED lighting for special effects. Decorative fixtures are employed in high end, themed dining venues, since they add a critical, character-bestowing level of detail, along with custom designed fixtures, which enable the firm to match their scale and finish seamlessly with the interior design program. Though color has its place in the total scheme, particularly in the lobby, bar and any thematic setting, the firm limits its presence on dining surfaces to showcase the cuisine like works

1, 4: Ruth's Chris Steakhouse, Sacramento, California, KITAbayashi Design Studio, architect; PHOTOGRAPHER, photographer.

2, 3, 5: Ruth's Chris Steakhouse, Roseville, California, KITAbayashi Design Studio, architect; PHOTOGRAPHER, photographer.

3

4

5

Fox & Fox Design

Hospitality/Restaurant

of art. Daylight, by contrast, plays a growing role for clients such as Ruth's Chris Steakhouse, which has evolved from one moderately-priced New Orleans restaurant founded in 1965 by Ruth Fertel to an upscale franchise whose modern vision of the steakhouse airy, open and daylit is flourishing in three California locations, Sacramento, Roseville, and Anaheim, all designed by KITAbayashi Design Studio, architect, and Fox & Fox Design, lighting designer. Adjacent to the trendy, new Shade Hotel, Petro's lures its own share of passersby with a warm, inviting interior of layered lighting featuring complementary backlit blue neon signage, Murano glass pendants with soft, diffuse incandescent lamps, and ivory candles prominently lining the walls. Though its scale and operations may be more modest than those of Ruth's Chris, the design by Tolkin & Associates Architecture, architect, and Fox & Fox Design, lighting designer, is no less professional. Guests feel the excitement as they enter, with adjustable MR-16 accent lamps casting light down the front trellis columns and planter boxes, announcing the start of a memorable dining experience.

1 - 3: Petro's Greek Cuisine and Lounge, Manhattan Beach, California, Tolkin & Associates Architecture, architect; John Fox, photographer.

Francis Krahe & Associates, Inc.

304 South Broadway
Suite 500
Los Angeles, CA 90013
213.617.0477
213.617.0482 (Fax)
www.fkaild.com

Francis Krahe & Associates, Inc.

Fresno Federal Courthouse
Fresno, California

A powerful symbol of justice as well as a practical venue, the new, nine-story, 456,000-square-foot Fresno Federal Courthouse, in Fresno, California, has been designed by Gruen Associates, Moore Ruble Yudell Architects, and Brayton Hughes Design Studios as architects and Francis Krahe & Associates as lighting designer to address its complex role in society. The symbolic and functional nature of its 25 courtrooms, 17 judges' chambers, galleries, main entrance, public lobby, and 3.9-acre, landscaped site is evident in the lighting for three key areas. Within the courthouse galleries, custom-designed glass lanterns mounted to window wall mullions create transparency to view judicial functions, display the sophistication of the architecture, and transform the building into a beacon at night. Large, multi-tiered lanterns within the public lobby reflect the space's monumental scale, supplemented by indirect light from fluorescent strips that highlight the ceiling's trellis frame. Courtroom lighting establishes a dignified setting with excellent visibility for participants, using T5 fluorescent sources below the center vault and at the perimeter of flanking soffits for general illumination, recessed halogen PAR38 lights to wash wood wall panels, provide key and fill light, and custom frosted-glass cylinder lanterns to reinforce the Stature of the court.

Francis Krahe & Associates, Inc.

Legacy Salmon Creek Hospital
Vancouver, Washington

1 - 7: **Legacy Salmon Creek Hospital,** Vancouver, Washington, Zimmer Gunsul Frasca Partnership, architect; Eckert & Eckert Photography, Frank Domin Photography, photographers.

As the first new hospital built for greater Portland in years, the new, 220-bed, six-story, 470,000-square-foot Legacy Salmon Creek Hospital, in Vancouver, Washington, combines the latest in medicine, technology and service within a sensitive healing environment. The full-service community hospital, designed by Zimmer Gunsul Frasca Partnership as architect and Francis Krahe & Associates as lighting designer, offers emergency services, labor/delivery, surgery, cancer care, cardiology, diagnostics and various other services. Its award-winning lighting design applies a comprehensive approach to lighting throughout the site, building exterior and hospital interior. For example, a metal halide pole system lights site roads and provides a formal structure to the campus, softly illuminating the streetscape leading to the entrance and main lobby, while a linear fluorescent system washes the frit glass walls of the second-level pedestrian bridge and visibly connects the parking, medical office building and hospital. Indoors, warm, domestic-quality lighting enables public areas such as the lobby, cafeteria, conference center and chapel to comfort patients and families. For acute care and intensive care patient rooms, family areas and waiting rooms, soft, indirect lighting counteracts and diminishes the need for direct lighting in procedures and examinations, accommodating the needs of patients, visitors and staff alike.

8

Francis Krahe & Associates, Inc.

The Shops at Tanforan
San Bruno, California

The redevelopment of The Shops at Tanforan, in San Bruno, California, designed by Altoon + Porter Architects as architect and Francis Krahe & Associates as lighting designer, gives San Francisco Peninsula families a shopping center with its own sophisticated character. The Shops at Tanforan houses over 100 established stores and restaurants, such as Barnes & Noble, BJ's Restaurant & Brewhouse, Old Navy, Guess, and Forever 21, within a structure containing over one million square feet of space, 105,000 square feet for public areas, and 72,000 square feet for entertainment, including a 20-screen, stadium-style cinema. To illuminate this volume, the lighting design must simultaneously differentiate individual areas while integrating them. The east court, the principal entry and pedestrian connection to El Camino Real, features post light fixtures. The lofty entry lobby, a transparent, three-story lantern, incorporates indirect cold cathode lighting for structure and roof deck with uplights suspended from ceiling panels. The west court, facing the entertainment facilities and BART station, glows under contrasting layers of colored ambient light. Subtle details, such as interior upper columns accented with surface-mounted uplights, and wall sconces that dramatize ceilings and their lighting reveals, complete the scheme.

1 - 6: The Shops at Tanforan, San Bruno, California, Altoon + Porter Architects, architect; Frank Domin Photography, photographer.

Francis Krahe & Associates, Inc.

Westfield Century City
Los Angeles, California

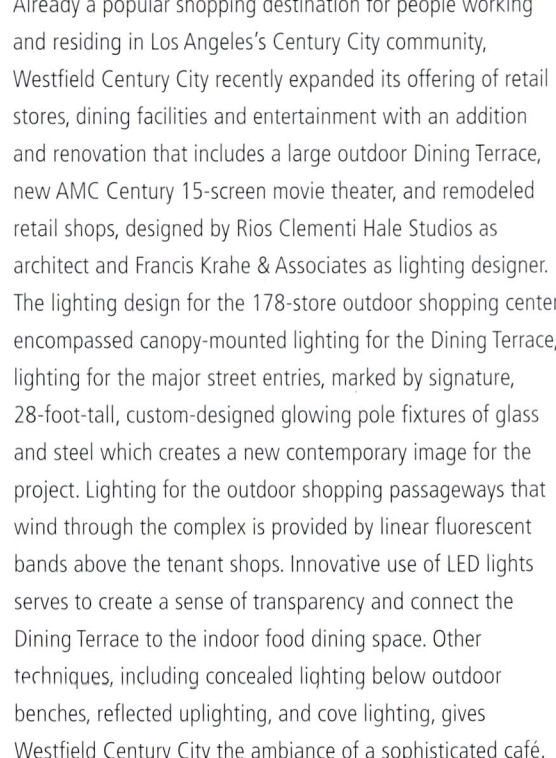

Already a popular shopping destination for people working and residing in Los Angeles's Century City community, Westfield Century City recently expanded its offering of retail stores, dining facilities and entertainment with an addition and renovation that includes a large outdoor Dining Terrace, new AMC Century 15-screen movie theater, and remodeled retail shops, designed by Rios Clementi Hale Studios as architect and Francis Krahe & Associates as lighting designer. The lighting design for the 178-store outdoor shopping center encompassed canopy-mounted lighting for the Dining Terrace, lighting for the major street entries, marked by signature, 28-foot-tall, custom-designed glowing pole fixtures of glass and steel which creates a new contemporary image for the project. Lighting for the outdoor shopping passageways that wind through the complex is provided by linear fluorescent bands above the tenant shops. Innovative use of LED lights serves to create a sense of transparency and connect the Dining Terrace to the indoor food dining space. Other techniques, including concealed lighting below outdoor benches, reflected uplighting, and cove lighting, gives Westfield Century City the ambiance of a sophisticated café.

1 - 5: Westfield Century City, Los Angeles, California, Rios Clementi Hale Studios, architect; Tom Bonner Photography, photographer.

Gallegos Lighting Design

Orlando, FL
Gallegos Lighting Design
a division of GRG INC.
2601 Westhall Lane
Maitland, FL 32751
321.263.0246
407.660.1161 (Fax)

San Francisco, CA
Gallegos Lighting Design
a division of GRG INC.
1306 Pomona Street
Suite 204
Crockett, CA 94525
510.787.0337
510.787.0339 (Fax)

San Diego, CA
Gallegos Lighting Design
a division of GRG INC.
5670 Oberlin Drive
San Diego, CA 92121
858.597.0555
858.597.0565 (Fax)

www.gallegoslighting.com

Gallegos Lighting Design

Themed Entertainment

Great themed entertainment not only seduces the guest the moment he or she enters its unique combination of architecture and theater, it creates an inviting and immersive experience that the guest wants to enjoy to the very last moment. Lighting design is essential for successful entertainment environments. In fact, clients compliment Gallegos Lighting Design for creating such outstanding lighting experiences at night that they feel they have paid for one park but received two. How are such results achieved? The key to success is a cohesive visual experience. Virtually every type of lamp is needed, for example, due to the detail required and the need for specialized control. Similarly, the entire spectrum of luminaires may be incorporated, particularly on large entertainment projects, where decorative fixtures must be consistent in style and details with the theme of the particular space. Attention must also be paid to color, a critical tool demanding careful use, daylight, the potential enemy of every controlled experience, and energy conservation, which can be promoted by local and park-wide control systems that monitor aesthetic balancing as well as energy consumption. When every detail is in place, however, the themed environment is unlike anything the guest has ever seen.

1, 4: **LEGOLAND California,** Carlsbad, California, Rouse Wyatt Design Group, project designer; photography courtesy of Gallegos Lighting Design.

2: **Warner Bros. Movie World Madrid,** Madrid, Spain, Warner Bros. Entertainment, project designer; photography courtesy of Warner Bros. International Recreation Enterprises.

3: **Dr. Jeekhan,** Tokyo, Japan, Dyflex Creation, project designer; photography courtesy of Gallegos Lighting Design.

Gallegos Lighting Design

In an age when "reality" is often anything but real, museums can distinguish themselves through immersive experiences that retain their focus on the true stories being told as well as the genuine artifacts on display. Gallegos Lighting Design finds that lighting styles and approaches can vary considerably among its museum projects, owing to the proliferating numbers and diverse goals of these institutions. Some require a traditional treatment, while others call for a more theatrical style. Not infrequently, projects even rely on the lighting itself to help create experiences that completely engulf guests. Although various lamps are used in museums, halogen fixtures tend to anchor most lighting designs, due to the need to create specific, controlled environments. Luminaires are subject to similar conditions, with a wide variety being used overall and track lines and fixtures being favored for practical reasons. As for such issues as color, daylight, and energy conservation, their applicability depends heavily on the

context. While color must support the experience being sought, daylight may be restricted to protect highly sensitive artifacts, and energy usage is subject to project-wide, automated control systems and careful lamp selection. Regardless of the setting, museum lighting gives reality the visibility it deserves.

1, 4: COSI, Columbus, Ohio, COSI Studios, exhibit designer; photography courtesy of Gallegos Lighting Design.

2: Southwest Museum, Los Angeles, California, Gruen & Associates, architect; Assassi Productions, photographer.

3: Golden State Museum, Sacramento, California, EHDD, architect; Tom Hartman & Associates, exhibit designer; Larry Hammerness Photography, photographer.

5: California Aerospace Museum, Los Angeles, California, Frank O. Gehry, architect; Joseph A. Wetzel Associates, exhibit designer; photography courtesy of Gallegos Lighting Design.

Gallegos Lighting Design

Aquaria

How do you welcome guests to the underwater world? The lighting design of the contemporary aquarium follows a two-stage approach. Exterior lighting, as created by Gallegos Lighting Design, is colorful and dramatic to focus guests' attention. However, interior lighting fulfills different goals: to assure and direct guests through the facility, provide naturalistic ambience for exhibits and displays, and acknowledge specific lighting factors that affect animal welfare. Lighting equipment likewise reflects the aquarium's unique conditions. High wattage metal halide lamps illuminate tank and other wet environments, exploiting their long life, intensity and color temperature, while dimmed halogen lamps give exhibit areas needed lower lighting levels. Luminaires follow similar criteria, with outdoor wet location, marine-grade metal halide fixtures appearing wherever water is involved, and track-mounted, adjustable accent fixtures and specialty theatrical projectors giving exhibit areas the definition they require. Color requires subtlety as well, involving the natural color temperature of lamps and color filters, to account for intended underwater color shifts and moods sought for specific dry exhibit areas, as does daylight, given its potential impact on highly regulated water temperatures and algae growth. Such complexities aside, growing public attendance strongly suggests that lighting design is truly enriching the aquarium experience.

1, 4, 5: Long Beach Aquarium, Long Beach, California, EHDD/HOK, associated architects; Joseph A. Weizel Associates, exhibit designer; Ronald Moore & Associates, photographer.

2, 3: Colorado Ocean Journey, Denver, Colorado, Joseph A. Weizel Associates, exhibit designer; Pat Gallegos, photographer.

6: Florida Aquarium, Tampa, Florida, EHDD/HOK, associated architects; Joseph A. Weizel Associates, exhibit designer; Pat Gallegos, photographer.

7: Monterey Bay Aquarium, Monterey, California, EHDD, architect; Aram Ebben, photographer.

1

Everyday concerns are forgotten when guests step inside the gaming environment, and the two-story, 130,000-square-foot renovation and expansion of the Argosy Casino, in Riverside, Missouri, aims at nothing less than transporting guests to an enchanted Mediterranean city where even the sky is entertaining. Indeed, fantasy presides over the rejuvenated casino, including its exterior facades and grounds, interior atria, restaurants, VIP lounges and gaming floors, designed by PGAV as architect, DesignPlan Inc. as project designer, and Gallegos Lighting Design as lighting designer. The initial mood is set by the exterior lighting, which illuminates fanciful towers and massive walls with crenellated parapets through a dynamic and appealing installation that features 837 fully programmable pencil strobes and produces a spectacular

nightly lighting show. Inside, the lighting works with the casino's intricately designed interiors to introduce a new and immersive experience for guests. While standard architectural lighting fixtures are used to great effect in the design, winner of a 2005 IES Award of Merit, state-of-the-art specialty systems, including programmable LEDs, fiber optics, theatrical color changing luminaires, and a sophisticated lighting control system, jointly dazzle guests with such sights as the soaring, 40,000-square-foot sky above the principal gaming area. Shouldn't guests enjoy a realistic night sky lighting show, complete with aurora borealis, at the Argosy Casino?

1 - 6: **Argosy Casino,** Riverside, Missouri, PGAV, architect; DesignPlan Inc., project designer; Aram Ebben, Pat Gallegos, photographers.

h.e. banks + associates

461 Second Street, #659
San Francisco, CA 94107
415.618.0855
415.618.0856 (Fax)
info@hebanks.com
www.hebanks.com

h.e. banks + associates

What could be more appropriate for the briefing centers Cisco Systems operates across the nation than an interactive lighting design, featuring dynamic, energy-efficient and color-changing lighting, that is applicable to different facilities? For Cisco Systems, a leader in networking equipment and management systems for the Internet, these high-tech conference centers are essential for showcasing equipment and services to clients' decision makers. The lighting design created by h.e. banks + associates for the renovated, 37,000-square-foot Executive Briefing Center, in San Jose, and the new, 5,000-square-foot Customer Briefing Centers, around the country, designed by Hellmuth Obata & Kassabaum, lets Cisco write custom-tailored light shows for LED ceilings, fluorescent ambient light, individual halogen spotlights and even LCD glass panels without an in-house lighting designer. In the Executive Briefing Center, Cisco employs a sophisticated architectural dimming system with user-friendly interface. In the smaller Customer Briefing Centers, a simpler system offers the same user interface for intuitive, everyday operation. Yet the elegance of the overall system doesn't come at the expense of individual spaces, including reception, demonstration hub, touchdown areas and conference rooms. The lighting acknowledges each space's function while maintaining a feeling of movement between exhibits not unlike an art gallery for e-commerce.

1, 2, 4, 5: **Cisco Systems,** Executive Briefing Center, San Jose, California, Hellmuth Obata & Kassabaum, architect; Peter Paige, photographer. 2006 IESNA Edwin F. Guth Memorial Award of Excellence for Interior Lighting Design.

3: **Cisco Systems,** Customer Briefing Center, New York, New York, Hellmuth Obata & Kassabaum, architect; Peter Paige, photographer. 2006 IESNA Edwin F. Guth Memorial Award of Excellence for Interior Lighting Design.

h.e. banks + associates

Customers and employees won't encounter canoes, rolling surf or boundless sky in American Savings Bank's flagship branch and executive offices in Honolulu. They may marvel, nevertheless, at how the two-level, 5,000-square-foot space, designed by Wimberly Allison Tong & Goo, architect, and h.e. banks + associates, lighting designer, evokes Hawaiian cultural themes without using literal images—and simultaneously provides lighting that meets and exceeds strict local energy codes. The award-winning lighting scheme is made possible by expert use of lighting technique. Fluorescent coves behind curving forms, for example, let ceiling soffits "float," as groups of luminous, cloud-like pendants hover over conference rooms. Of course, the design is functional too. While daylight is filtered through wood lattice panels to control the sun's glare, custom luminaires suspended in openings in the sweeping canopy provide

task lighting and signal teller availability by blinking, using incandescent lamps for the on/off effect, and fluorescent trough lights regressed in the rear of the canopy meet the recommended IESNA 500 lux for fast, accurate transactions and glare-free illumination on teller screens. The harmonious integration of light and architecture combine with a responsible approach to energy and maintenance to celebrate the local ownership and community commitment of Hawaii's third-largest financial institution.

1, 3, 4, 5: American Savings Bank, Flagship Branch, Honolulu, Hawaii, Wimberly Allison Tong & Goo, architect; Jody Pritchard, photographer. 2004 IESNA Illumination Design Award for Outstanding Achievement in Lighting Design.

2, 6: American Savings Bank, Executive Offices, Honolulu, Hawaii, Wimberly Allison Tong & Goo, architect; Jody Pritchard, photographer. 2004 IESNA Illumination Design Award for Outstanding Achievement in Lighting Design.

h.e. banks + associates

RayKo Photo Center

Long a community hub for Bay Area photographers, San Francisco's RayKo Photo Center recently reopened in a two-floor, 12,000-square-foot space converted from an existing warehouse, designed by Neil Schwartz, architect, and h.e. banks + associates, lighting designer, that is defined by its award-winning lighting. The new facility, which offers digital imaging and scanning tools, rental darkrooms and studios, a retail space promoting the work of regional artists, and a gallery, bases its design on principles central to photography—the control and modulation of light. With the center of the main floor occupied by the Lightbox/Darkbox, a building within a building, the project introduces an abstract, glowing icon for the Center enclosing such "dark" functions as communal enlarging stations, rental laboratories and large format mural studio. By contrast, the exterior of the volume, which organizes the balance of the space into four distinct functional zones for "light" activities, namely retail gallery, exhibition gallery, layout and print check, is dramatized by a 200-foot-long continuous illuminated parapet wall of translucent PVC stretch fabric that fills the open space with a soft and abstract light. By encouraging visual and social interaction, the lighting preserves the open, communal nature that endears the Center to its users.

1 - 5: RayKo Photo Center, San Francisco, California, Neil Schwartz, architect; Anna Case-Hoffmeister, Gary Hesse, Monica Nelson, photographers. 2006 AIA San Francisco Merit Award.

h.e. banks + associates

Magnet

Creating an interesting lighting design in a community space with a tight budget and limited tool box calls for keen problem solving and a commitment to the client's goals. Fortunately, the result can be fresh and inspiring, as shown in Magnet, a health clinic and community center for San Francisco's gay community in the legendary Castro neighborhood. This one-floor, 1,100-square-foot renovation of existing commercial space, designed pro bono by Rachel Hamilton, of Hamilton & Company, architect, David Meckley of MK Think, interior designer, and h.e. banks & associates, lighting designer, serves numerous functions besides health and social services, such as book readings, art exhibits, town hall meetings and social events. The lighting for these activities, comprising an ambient luminous ceiling and adjustable, low-voltage rail system, makes the most of equipment and wattage to meet California's Title 24 energy code, accommodate structure, and minimize costs. Inexpensive T5 striplights backlight the undulating ceiling panels. Standard fixtures such as industrial sign lighters, monopoints and low-voltage rail are carefully positioned to emit high quality light, free of distracting reflection and glare. Evenly distributed general light levels of approximately 300 lux enable Magnet to serve various activities and shine a welcoming beacon into the community.

1 - 5: **Magnet,** San Francisco, California, Rachel Hamilton, Hamilton & Company, architect; David Meckley of MK Think, interior designer; David Toerge, photographer. Architectural Lighting's 2004 Light + Architecture Design Awards, Best Design on a Budget; 2004 IESNA Illumination Design Award for Outstanding Achievement in Lighting Design.

h.e. banks + associates

Four Seasons Penthouse

In a modern, 2,500-square-foot penthouse residence, located atop the Four Seasons Hotel near the San Francisco Museum of Modern Art, architecture and lighting are seamlessly integrated in a design by Gemmill Design, architect, Gary Hutton Design, interior designer, and h.e. banks + associates, lighting designer that could represent a dream come true for many an art collector. A battery of lamps and luminaires is employed to give the client an environment for everyday living, entertaining and developing an artistic vision, offering layers of light for general activities and the ability to adapt to an ever-changing modern art collection. Above the dining room table, for example, a vented recessed channel houses low-voltage strip lights for ambient light and a recessed busway for accent lighting on the table. A similar light slot is visible

in the living room, where four square recessed boxes house adjustable accent lights for art on the columns. Architectural slots in the kitchen use dimmable fluorescent lamps for ambient uplighting and meet California's Title 24 energy code. Blurring traditional roles, h.e. banks + associates even developed custom lighting details tailored to the architectural design, ensuring that lighting would blend with art and architecture in this distinctive installation.

1 - 5: Penthouse Residence at the Four Seasons Hotel, San Francisco, California, Gemmill Design, architect; Gary Hutton Design, interior designer; Jody Pritchard, photographer. 2006 IALD Award of Merit; 2006 IESNA Illumination Design Award for Outstanding Achievement in Lighting Design.

h.e. banks + associates

Mount Tiburon Residence

The challenge: Make the rooms in a remodeled Arts & Crafts home featuring black floors, open, 20-foot-high wood ceilings and large windows feel welcoming while highlighting the art collection. In collaborating with Buttler Armsden Architects, architect, and Stephen Miller Design, interior designer, on the Mount Tiburon residence, in Tiburon, California, h.e. banks + associates, lighting designer, has found the lighting solution in clever architectural modifications and careful placement of luminaires that preserve the home's aesthetics and create warm lighting for comfortable living. The existing ceiling structure provided a way to mount fixtures, through the closing of the gap between the lower parallel truss chords with a continuous regressed cap, permitting low-voltage linear uplights to be mounted with a raceway to conceal the wiring. As a result, multiple layers of light can be delivered and adjusted in various ways, with the upper chords receiving track with adjustable AR111 lamps for tight beam control, and the lower beams getting UV-filtered MR16 lamps to focus on art. Though most of the lighting is integrated with the architecture, a linear, luminous pendant, modified to include an interior low-voltage striplight, has also been installed for its scale, enriching the home while respecting its character.

Horton Lees Brogden Lighting Design Inc.

New York
200 Park Ave. South
Suite 1401
New York, NY 10003
212.674.5580
212.254.2712 (Fax)

San Francisco
300 Brannan Street
Suite 212
San Francisco, CA 94107
415.348.8273
415.348.8298 (Fax)

Los Angeles
8580 Washington Blvd.
Culver City, CA 90232
310.837.0929
310.837.0902 (Fax)

www.HLBlighting.com

Horton Lees Brogden Lighting Design Inc.

Performing Arts

What we see influences how we perceive and experience our environment, and the lighting of performance spaces can demonstrate the phenomenon of vision in unforgettable ways. The visual experience starts with the magic of light on or from within the building, and Horton Lees Brogden Lighting Design likes to create a glowing façade, dazzling lobby or dynamic, color-changing palette on the exterior to set the stage for what's to come inside. Since patrons should be able to see and be seen, the lighting of the house is as important as the lighting of the stage. In fact, patrons are as much a part of concert hall events as performers. The firm's approach to lighting varies with the space, being discretely integrated with the architecture to inject a sense of magic, or used as a visible light element to provide rhythm, glow or sparkle. Lighting that introduces color must be applied selectively to avoid upstaging events. In selecting light sources, the firm usually chooses incandescent lamps for dimming capabilities and lack of audible harmonics that could interfere with the acoustics. But selections must also acknowledge energy conservation and long service life, because budget and maintenance are essential to every show.

1: Utah State University, Manon Caine Russell Kathryn Caine Wanlass Performance Hall, Logan, Utah, Sasaki Associates, Inc., architect; ©Robert Benson, photographer.

2, 3: Williams College, Williams College '62 Center for Theatre & Dance, Williamstown, Massachusetts, William Rawn Associates, Architects Inc., architect; ©Robert Benson, photographer.

4: Seattle Opera House, Marion Oliver McCaw Hall, Seattle, Washington, LMN Architects, architect; ©Arch Photo, Eduard Hueber, photographer. IES IIDA Award of Merit, IES IIDA Lumen West Award of Excellence.

5: Benaroya Symphony Hall, Seattle, Washington, LMN Architects, architect; ©Lara Swimmer, photographer. IES IIDA Award of Merit.

6: Denver Performing Arts Center, Ellie Caulkins Opera House, Denver, Colorado, Semple Brown Design, architect; ©Ron Pollard, photographer.

Horton Lees Brogden Lighting Design Inc.

Commercial Exterior/Interior

Lighting plays a critical role in branding exterior and interior commercial environments across skylines and highways in urban and rural areas, and Horton Lees Brogden Lighting Design uses it to draw focus and establish drama as well as support functionality. By combining their experience, technical skills, and hands on approach to develop successful lighting for commerce, the firm's innovative design work complements the visual environment. Yet, besides achieving a quality of lighting that enhances the public image of a commercial facility, the lighting design must maximize the effectiveness of both the exterior and interior, and contribute to the well-being of occupants and visitors.

To support business transactions, good lighting will incorporate standard materials and methods that are cost-effective, easy to maintain, and readily replaceable, whenever feasible. Signature lighting should be used only in areas that make sense, given the overall design and hierarchy of the space. Above all other considerations, lighting design should balance the client's need to express the unique qualities of the organization with its employees' need to perform job tasks quickly, accurately and comfortably. The firm believes good lighting can do all this—and unify the facility, create visual variety, and signal changes in activities at the same time.

1: Caltrans District 7 Headquarters, Los Angeles, California, Morphosis, architect; Keith Sonnier, neon sculpture artist; ©Mark Dell'Aquila, Eagle-Eye Images.com, photographer. IES IIDA Award of Merit, IES IIDA Lumen West Award of Excellence.

2: MTV On Line, New York, New York, Kiss + Zwigard Architects, architect; ©Catherine Tighe, photographer.

3: MetLife Tower, New York, New York, Building Conservation Associates Inc., architect; ©Elliott Kaufman, photographer. IES IIDA Lumen Citation.

4: Novartis Institute for Functional Genomics, La Jolla, California, NBBJ, architect; ©Tim Griffith, photographer. IES IIDA Golden Gate Section Award.

5: Moët Hennessy, New York, New York, TPG Architecture, architect; ©Adrian Wilson, New York, photographer.

Horton Lees Brogden Lighting Design Inc. Public Buildings/Spaces

Public buildings and spaces resemble their counterparts in the private sector in many ways, but they differ in one fundamental and inescapable manner. They must endure for decades—well beyond the attention span of the corporate world—supporting public activities and expressing the civic values they symbolize. Designing lighting for public facilities is a challenge Horton Lees Brogden Lighting Design resolves with knowledge, talent and experience. The firm strives for sensitive solutions that celebrate the qualities of specific places and the citizens who build them—the magnificent details of an historic façade, the sleek planes of glass, metal and other modern materials defining a contemporary building, or the civility and charm of a public park—while serving the public's needs. Typically, the lighting must meet complex goals that reflect a multitude of public concerns. In public streetscape projects, for example, lighting must be provided for pedestrians while night sky light pollution is minimized or eliminated through the use or design of appropriate optics, lamps and strategic locations for equipment. Whatever the prevailing conditions may be, Horton Lees Brogden Lighting Design works closely with the architectural team to realize the potential of public art, landscape features, fountains and architectural forms to be illuminated at night.

1: Pier One, Adaptive Reuse, San Francisco, California, SMWM, architect, Tom Eliot Fisch, associate architect; ©Richard Barnes, photographer. IES IIDA Award of Merit.

2: Santana Row, San Jose, California, Street-Works, architect; ©Horton Lees Brogden Lighting Design Inc., photographer.

3: Los Angeles City Hall, Exterior Historic Renovation, Los Angeles, California, Project Restore, Antieri Haloossim & Mattingly Consulting Engineers, project team; ©Tom Bonner Photography, photographer. IES IIDA Award of Merit, IES IIDA Lumen West Award of Excellence.

4, 7: San Francisco City Hall, Exterior and Interior Renovation, San Francisco, California, Heller•Manus Architects, MBT Architecture, Komorous-Towey Architects, FMG Architects, San Francisco Bureau of Architecture, design team; ©Robert Canfield Photography (4), ©Jay Graham (7), photographers. IALD Award of Merit, IES IIDA Waterbury Award of Merit, IES IIDA EPRI Award of Merit, IES IIDA Guth Award of Merit.

5: The National World War II Memorial, Washington, D.C., Friedrich St. Florian Architect, Leo A Daly, Oehme, van Sweden & Associates, Inc., Kaskey Studio, Inc., design team; ©Brett Drury Architectural Photography, photographer. IES IIDA Lumen Award of Merit.

6: Nasher Sculpture Center, Garden, Dallas, Texas, Peter Walker and Partners, landscape architect; ©Peter Walker and Partners, photographer.

6

7

Horton Lees Brogden Lighting Design Inc.   Transportation

Airports and mass transit environments can be daunting, confusing and often frustrating for passengers, who arrive with individual wants and needs—plus levels of tolerance, comprehension and motivation that mark them as seasoned road warriors or occasional travelers. Thus, the lighting created by Horton Lees Brogden Lighting Design for transportation space responds thoughtfully to the central human themes of vision, namely what we experience, how we experience it, and why we experience it. Lighting is used subliminally to move people through spaces, create visual clues to direct them, and warn of transitional areas. Fortunately, there are numerous ways for lighting to communicate to passengers. The type of lighting used, for example, can celebrate the architecture, complement natural light, serve as a beacon for arriving passengers, and establish clarity so that graphics can be readily understood. The color of lighting is often a way to distinguish vertical and horizontal circulation to gates, platforms or parking. As with all of its projects, the firm prides itself on utilizing energy-efficient systems and a minimal number of lamp types that will survive the tests of time, budget and maintenance that determine the longevity of transportation spaces. Good lighting will help keep transportation facilities in motion.

1: Los Angeles Metro Rail Vermont/Santa Monica Station, Los Angeles, California, Ellerbe Becket, architect; ©Timothy Hursley, Photography, IES IIDA Award of Merit, U.S. Dept. of Transportation Design for Transportation National Merit Award.

2, 4: Ronald Reagan Washington National Airport, Washington, D.C., Pelli Clarke Pelli Architects, Leo A Daly, Pierce Goodwin Alexander & Linville, architects; ©Jeff Goldberg/Esto Photographics, photographer. IES IIDA EPRI Award of Excellence, U.S. Dept. of Transportation Design for Transportation National Honor Award.

3: Ben Gurion International Airport, Airside Terminal, Tel Aviv, Israel, Moshe Safdie & Associates, architect; ©Alan Karchmer/Esto Photographics, photographer.

John Levy Lighting Productions

The World Trade Center Building
350 S. Figueroa Street
Suite 127
Los Angeles, CA 90071
213.629.9949
213.629.9969 (Fax)
www.jllp.net

John Levy Lighting Productions

Resorts, Casinos & Hotels

People flock to resorts, casinos and hotels that offer fresh, creative and pleasurable ways to escape from everyday cares. John Levy Lighting Productions makes innovative use of new and existing technologies to create signature lighting installations for these projects. Since each installation is unique, the firm designs solutions to enhance the guest experience by harmonizing with the architecture and interior design. The primary focus of any gaming and hospitality development is obviously on major guest areas. Nevertheless, the firm takes care that all secondary areas receive appropriate levels of ambiance. So while a casino hotel's main entry might incorporate a "wow" feature using lighting, video

and musical arrangement to establish a must-see spectacle for guests, its other attractions will also be designed to draw guests at appropriate times. Casinos, for example, require tight control of lighting sources with low glare, restaurants may be softly illuminated for intimate dining, bar lounges can sparkle brightly to support spirited conversations, and entertainment areas often project multiple personalities to accommodate varied activities, from a quiet drink at a bar to a lively gathering in a major dance club space. Even exteriors can bolster a project's identity through outdoor lighting that seduces guests at nightfall.

1: Green Valley Ranch Casino Resort, Henderson, Nevada, Friedmutter Group, Las Vegas, architect; Scott Avjian Design, Inc., interior designer; Friedmutter Group, Las Vegas, photographer.

2: Harrah's Poydras Hotel, New Orleans, Louisiana, Manning Architects, Marnell Corrao Associates, architects; Marnell Corrao Associates, interior designer; Peter Malinowski, photographer.

3: Green Valley Ranch Casino Resort, Henderson, Nevada, Friedmutter Group, Las Vegas, architect; Avery Brooks & Associates, interior designer; Friedmutter Group, Las Vegas, photographer.

4: Caesar's Palace, Las Vegas, Nevada, Wimberly Allison Tong & Goo, architect; Archavision, design consultant; John Levy Lighting Productions, photographer.

John Levy Lighting Productions

Once separate and distinct enterprises, bars and restaurants are becoming synonymous or sharing the same space. But the various spaces and activities they sustain invariably serve different and often conflicting purposes during the course of the day, week and season, making control of the lighting environment in a bar or restaurant critical to operations. Optimum lighting during lunch, for example, may be inappropriate for dinner. And the right setting for intimate dining is unlikely to satisfy a high-energy dance club. To give bars and restaurants the versatility they need, John Levy Lighting Productions uses multiple types of lamps, luminaires, controls and other equipment, such as decorative lighting to provide sparkle and visual interest, low-voltage downlighting for ambient level and accenting art and artifacts, and LED color changing, moving lights, and pattern projectors. Lighting's impact on the character and perception of space can mean the difference between day and night.

1: Green Valley Ranch Casino Resort, Drop Bar, Henderson, Nevada, Architropolis, architect; Friedmutter Group, Las Vegas, interior designer; Friedmutter Group, Las Vegas, photographer.

2: Harrah's Poydras Hotel, New Orleans, Louisiana, Manning Architects, Marnell Corrao Associates, architects; Marnell Corrao Associates, interior designer; Peter Malinowski, photographer.

3: Harrah's Casino, Masquerade Bar, New Orleans, Louisiana, Wimberly Allison Tong & Goo, John Levy Lighting Productions, interior designers; John Levy Lighting Productions, photographer.

4: Green Valley Ranch Casino Resort, Whiskey Sky Bar, Henderson, Nevada, Friedmutter Group, Las Vegas, architect; Architropolis, interior designer; Friedmutter Group, Las Vegas, photographer.

5: Aladdin Casino & Resort, Las Vegas, Nevada, RTKL, architect and interior designer; Tokistar, photographer.

John Levy Lighting Productions

Corporate Offices

There is often more to corporate offices than meets the eye. Not only does office lighting support the tasks being performed by employees and enhance the architecture and interior design, it can play a major role in projecting the corporate identity to employees and visitors alike. This role is often unavoidable, since many businesses lease space in buildings that are seldom designed to their specific requirements. Besides developing an appropriate visual image for the client, John Levy Lighting Productions devises lighting solutions for activities that typically include both individual and group work with a broad spectrum of information technologies. Good office lighting means more than task lighting, however. To a general ambiance generated by electric sources and available daylight, the firm adds highlights for artwork, furniture groupings, and company displays or icons, using this technique to introduce visual variety and guide employees and visitors from entry spaces to their destinations. Good office lighting is not dull lighting.

1: Caesar's Palace, Executive Office, Las Vegas, Nevada, Marnell Corrao, architect and interior designer; John Levy Lighting Productions, photographer.

2: Parkview Square, Singapore, DP Architects Pte Ltd, Singapore, architect; Archavision, design consultant; John Levy Lighting Productions, photographer.

3: Hanmoo Convention Center, Singapore, Nadel Architects, architect; Poongjin Interior Designer, Inc., interior designer; John Levy Lighting Productions, photographer.

John Levy Lighting Productions

Exteriors

Pedestrians, motorists and airline passengers cannot help noticing that nighttime lighting of the built environment is becoming increasingly common, sophisticated and effective. For facility owners and operators, the illumination of exteriors of buildings and such outdoor structures and spaces as parking facilities, bridges, stairs, roads, sidewalks, parks and signs is a means of establishing spatial orientation, increasing market share, and enhancing safety and security. The challenges of exterior lighting that John Levy Lighting Productions resolves for clients thus address a diversity of issues. For example, visibility must be maintained from multiple viewing locations near and afar without overwhelming viewers close to or inside the structure. A nighttime identity must be convincingly established through the use of color, articulating

1: Moana Hotel, Honolulu, Hawaii, Virginia Murison, AIA, architect and interior designer; John Levy Lighting Productions, photographer.

2: Watergarden, Wilshire Boulevard, Los Angeles, California, Maclare Vasquez, architect and interior designer; Biaggio Guerra, photographer.

3: Cache Creek Casino, Cache Creek, California, Friedmutter Group, Las Vegas, architect and interior designer; Peter Malinowski, photographer.

4: Bally's Casino Hotel, Las Vegas, Nevada, Friedmutter Group, Las Vegas, architect; Allen Photography, photographer.

5: Green Valley Ranch Casino Resort, Henderson, Nevada, Friedmutter Group, Las Vegas, architect; Friedmutter Group, Las Vegas, photographer.

4

5

111

John Levy Lighting Productions

Exteriors

architectural details, animated lighting or lighting intensity. Lamps and fixtures must enjoy a long service life to withstand extreme environmental conditions and minimize costly, time-consuming maintenance procedures. With work and play becoming 24-hour phenomena, businesses and institutions want to keep the spotlight on their activities long after the sun goes down.

1: **Parkview Square,** Singapore, DP Architects Pte Ltd, Singapore, architect; Archavision, design consultant; John Levy Lighting Productions, photographer.

2: **Stratosphere Tower,** Las Vegas, Nevada, Gary Nelson, architect; John Levy Lighting Productions, photographer.

3: **Streets of the World,** MCA/Universal City, Hollywood, California, MCA/Universal City P&D, architect; John Levy Lighting Productions, photographer.

Lang Lighting Design, Inc.

120 Knox Place
4645 N. Central Expressway
Dallas, TX 75205
214.780.0700
214.780.0704 (Fax)
www.langlighting.com

Lang Lighting Design, Inc.

Hospitality

Four Seasons Hotel Doha
Doha, Qatar

Designing illumination for the world's finest hotels calls for top technical skills and artistic talent—plus a genuine understanding of local cultures and ways of doing business. For Lang Lighting Design, all these resources contribute to successful projects such as the 232-room Four Seasons Hotel Doha, a recent addition to the growing population of world-class hotels in Doha, capital city of Qatar in the Arabian Gulf. The scope of the assignment was to light the public spaces, such as the main lobby, Il Teatro italian restaurant, cigar bar lounge, and the grand lobby lounge, all designed by Frank Nicholson, Inc. The goal of the assignment was to use locally sourced equipment and lamps while maintaining the requirements of

a five-star hotel. To meet the goal, Lang Lighting Design took the time to understand the culture of Qatar and how Qataris do business, and established relationships that went the extra mile to get what was needed, including state-of-the-art control technology, to complete the project. Not surprisingly, the Four Seasons Hotel Doha has won such distinctions as the *Conde Nast* 2006 Hot List of New Hotels, *Conde Nast* 2006 Editors Choice award for best hotels, and Gallivants Choice 2006.

1 - 4: **Four Seasons Hotel Doha,** Doha, Qatar, Frank Nicholson, Inc., interior designer; Peter Vitale, photographer.

114

115

Lang Lighting Design, Inc.

Hospitality

Four Seasons Resort Scottsdale at Troon North
Scottsdale, Arizona

What makes an outdoor reception or dining al fresco seem special? Hospitality businesses integrate their outdoor spaces with their indoor activities to host everyday services and special events—given favorable site and climatic conditions, of course—because contact with the world beyond their walls intensifies the guests' senses and expands the boundaries of their perception. But integrating indoor and outdoor facilities takes care, and the appropriate lighting design may impose special precautions not encountered in interior installations. Such has been the case for the renovation and addition to the Four Seasons Resort Scottsdale at Troon North, in Scottsdale, Arizona, designed by Hill Glazier Architects, architect, and Brennan Beer Gorman Monk, interior designer, with Lang Lighting Design as lighting designer. Lighting the project at this five-star, 210-room resort, encompassing remodeled ballrooms and spa, new pre-function terrace, and new event lawn, fire ring and landscape sculpture, has required compliance with restrictive ordinances limiting exterior lighting, as well as technical skill to balance changing lighting levels indoors and outdoors. The successful lighting solution uses low-voltage accent lighting to highlight specific features in the landscape rather than blanket the exterior area, giving guests adequate visibility without obscuring the magnificent nighttime sky over the Sonoran Desert.

1 - 4: **Four Seasons Resort Scottsdale at Troon North,** Scottsdale, Arizona, Hill Glazier Architects, architect; Brennan Beer Gorman Monk, interior designer; Andy Lang, AIA, IALD, photographer.

Lang Lighting Design, Inc.

Corporate
UBS Financial Services
Houston, Texas

Public areas in corporate offices put businesses on display before their vendors and customers. To present a positive image before visitors to these areas, architects, interior designers and lighting designers strive to express the best qualities of their space, form and materials. Numerous technical, financial and aesthetic issues must inevitably be resolved along the way, however. Consider the recently completed office of UBS Financial Services, in Houston, Texas, designed by Interior Architects, architect, with Lang Lighting Design as lighting designer. To light the facility, which includes a spacious reception area with rusticated stone walls as well as general office space, and to do so in compliance with an extremely restrictive energy code, Lang Lighting Design has specified PAR 20 curved cove lighting fixtures for cove lighting above the stone walls, and T5 direct/indirect lighting in 2x2 fixtures that require only one lamp per fixture in general office space, thanks to newly developed direct/indirect fluorescent fixtures with meso-optic lenses.. Not only does the lighting design meet the energy code's standards, it portrays the reception area as bold, dynamic and attractive, giving visitors an inspiring first glimpse of the Houston office for one of the world's leading financial firms.

1 - 3: UBS Financial Services, Houston, Texas, Interior Architects, architect; Mark Scheyer, Inc., photographer.

Lang Lighting Design, Inc.

Residential
Camp Menehune
Athens, Texas

1

Art collectors developing residences to showcase their works of art present a special challenge as well as a rare opportunity to architects, interior designers and lighting designers. Imagine creating a museum-quality environment with the appropriate amenities and personal details to call it a home. The rewards of good coordination among members of a capable design team plus intensive, hands-on site coordination of a major residential design project are evident at Camp Menehune, an notable private residence in Athens, Texas, that has been remodeled by Staffelbach Design Associates, Inc., interior designer, with Lang Lighting Design as lighting designer. To execute the highly sophisticated lighting solution that brings out the rich colors in the home's fabrics and artwork,

Lang Lighting Design has employed MR-16 lamps for all accenting, A-lamp down lights for general illumination, a state-of-the-art lighting control system, and decorative lighting fixtures that are integral to the interior design. Residences that respond so superbly to the needs and wants of families come about largely through the cooperative efforts of architects, interior designers and lighting designers, and Camp Menehune shows it.

1 - 7: Camp Menehune, Athens, Texas, Staffelbach Design Associates, Inc., interior designer; Andy Lang, AIA, IALD, and Kellie Lang, photographers.

119

Lang Lighting Design, Inc.

Residential
Meaders Residence
Dallas, Texas

Positioning the lighting fixtures in a sleek, contemporary residence can be complicated by the understandable desire for concealed and/or minimally detailed lighting sources. However, Lang Lighting Design does not find that this requirement precludes superior lighting design. A good example is the Meaders Residence, in Dallas, a modern, two-story structure of stone, metal and glass designed by Bernbaum Magadini Architects, architect, and Patrick McElwee Interior Design, interior designer, with Lang Lighting Design as lighting designer. Since the client owns an extensive art collection, fine furnishings and a home with such dramatic architectural details as interior walls of stone and two-story-high spaces, the lighting design focuses on highlighting them with MR-16 lamps, A-lamp down lights and PAR-20 lamps that graze the stone work. Lighting fixtures chosen for this installation are minimal in appearance to complement the architecture, and their restraint extends to their energy consumption, enabling the lighting design to meet the latest energy code requirements for residential construction. It's an ideal example of how less can be more in modern residential design.

1 - 3: Meaders Residence, Dallas, Texas, Bernbaum Magadini Architects, architect; Patrick McElwee Interior Design, interior designer; Charles Smith, photographer.

Lightbrigade

70 Orchard Park Blvd.
Toronto, ON M4L 3E2
416.698.9899
416.698.3783 (Fax)
www.lightbrigade.ca

Lightbrigade

Retail

Crucial to successful retail illumination, notes Lightbrigade, is establishing a hierarchy of merchandise. The variance between feature displays, general merchandise and circulation areas can dictate the quality of both the retailer as well as the merchandise. Typically higher quality retailers employ less ambient light and higher contrast. Vertical illumination is critical for all elements of retail and well-lighted perimeter wall displays help draw customers into the store. Special features such as lighted niches, display cases or focal displays with light integration add visual interest. To highlight product, spot lamps excel in creating high contrast ratios between product and surroundings with little light bleed. Aluminum backed MR-16's are preferred as accent lights for high-end clientele, since they do not cast colored light on the ceilings compromising the interior finishes. For mid-level retailers, appropriate lamps include both PAR metal halide and halogen, MR-16's for merchandise and compact fluorescent for fill light. Linear fluorescents are incorporated into wall displays and ceiling coves while LED's are becoming prevalent in feature elements. Both energy efficiency and CRI are taken into consideration when selecting sources. The function of retail illumination is to draw focus to the product and heighten the visual experience while complimenting the interior design.

1, 4, 5, 6: La Maison Simons, Laval, QC; Watt International Inc., designers; Richard Johnson, www.interiorimages.ca, photography.

2: Brown Thomas & Co., Dublin, Ireland; burdifilek, designers; Ben Rahn/A-Frame, photography.

3: Holt Renfrew, Bloor Street, Toronto, ON; burdifilek, designers; Ben Rahn/A-Frame, photography.

3

4

5

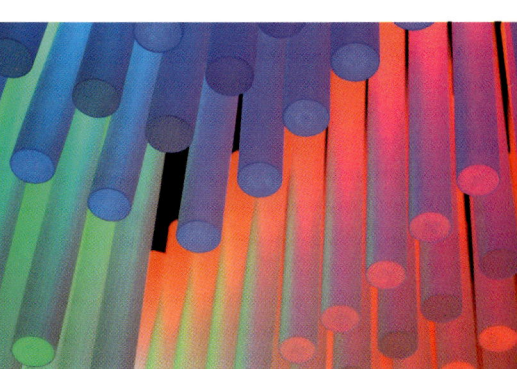

6

Lightbrigade

Health Care

Given lighting's increasingly important role in healthcare design, Lightbrigade works closely with architects and designers, incorporating quality, energy efficient lighting into architectural elements or details to produce comforting health care environments. The firm employs indirect luminaires and special backlighting techniques to create diffuse and glare-free illumination that is especially appreciated in spaces where patients must recline or lie down. Prominent in healthcare design is the integration of daylight. Wherever possible, the lighting design strives to recreate that sense of daylight during overcast days or evenings. Daylight is also valued for energy conservation as well as patient and staff well-being. Naturally lit transitional or circulation spaces have their artificial lighting systems controlled by light sensors, reducing or extinguishing light output as required. Canadian hospitals are government run, imposing strict guidelines that limit lamps to highly efficient sources, primarily linear and compact fluorescent. Metal halide lamps are often employed in double height spaces while low voltage accent lighting is reserved for key areas. Critical to lamp selection are lamps with superior color rendition across the spectrum. This allows health care workers to properly assess patient wellness. Limited numbers of lamp types are specified per project to ensure ease of lamp storage and maintenance.

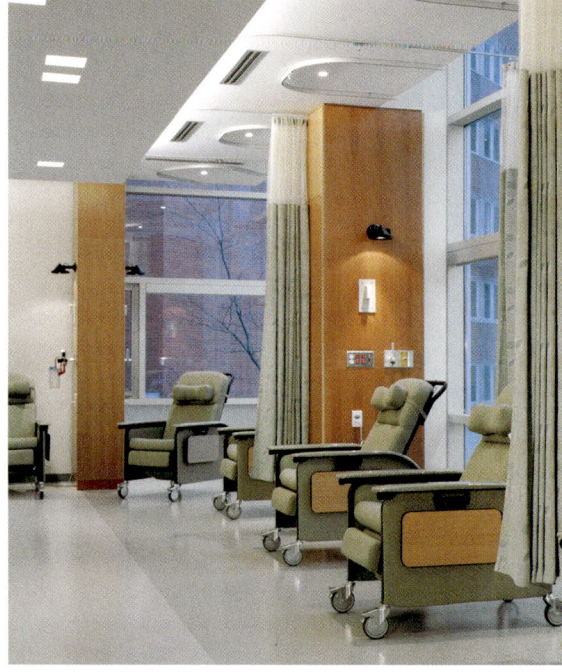

1: **Windsor Regional Cancer Centre,** radiation therapy treatment room, Kitchener, ON; Vermeulen/Hind Architects, architect; Ben Rahn/ A-Frame, photography.

2: **Grand River Regional Cancer Centre,** chemotherapy treatment room, Kitchener, ON; Vermeulen/Hind Architects, architect; Ben Rahn/ A-Frame, photography.

3: **Grand River Regional Cancer Centre,** radiation treatment room corridor, Kitchener, ON; Vermeulen/Hind Architects, architect; Ben Rahn/ A-Frame, photography.

Lightbrigade

Corporate

How should the business environment be lighted? The style of lighting Lightbrigade creates for corporate spaces depends wholly on the interior design style created by the architect or interior designer. Lightbrigade's high-end projects call for lighting that suits the aesthetics of the interior design, offering visual performance and interest while promoting energy efficiency and ease of maintenance. Taking this criteria into consideration, the lighting of general or personal office spaces often combines both task and ambient systems. Wall illumination is often used to offer a greater sense of brightness in a space, permitting overall illumination levels to be reduced. Special consideration is given to main boardrooms of most corporate offices. These spaces serve as

meeting rooms, reception spaces as well as video-conferencing suites – all of which require lighting systems that are at cross purposes to each other. The key is an aesthetic yet highly flexible system offering both horizontal and vertical light levels when required. For compliance with ASHRAE, high efficiency fluorescent lamps, often T5, are used for their very slim luminaire profiles. Well placed halogen sources highlight features. Where an abundance of usable daylight is available at window walls, sophisticated shade systems combined with light sensing controls are employed for energy savings.

1: **Sterner Automation,** industrial office, Toronto, ON; Cooper-Slipper Design, designer; Patrick Kennedy, www.pkphotographer.com, photography.

2: **InterContinental Hotel Toronto Centre,** video-conferencing centre, Toronto, ON; Elsie Cheng Design, designer; Michael Mahovlich photography.

3: **Toronto Dominion Bank Executive Offices,** waiting area, Toronto, ON; Figure 3, designers; Richard Johnson, www.interiorimages.ca, photography.

4: **Toronto Dominion Bank Executive Offices,** corridor gallery, Toronto, ON; Figure 3, designers; Richard Johnson, www.interiorimages.ca, photography.

Lightbrigade

Residential

1: **Contemporary Residence,** stair, Toronto, ON; Marnie Mancini Interior Design, designer; Patrick Kennedy, www.pkphotographer.com, photography.

2: **Private Residence,** living/dining room, Canada; Lynn Appleby & Ingrid Kost, designers; Patrick Kennedy, www.pkphotographer.com, photography.

3: **Traditional Residence,** dining room, Toronto, ON; McCormack/Design Arc, designer; Patrick Kennedy, www.pkphotographer.com, photography.

4: **Contemporary Residence,** living room, Toronto, ON, Marnie Mancini Interior Design, designer; Patrick Kennedy, www.pkphotographer.com, photography.

Homes with a dynamic balance of light and shadow are homes with successful lighting. Lightbrigade believes that lighting elements should either be prominent feature elements tied to the interior design such as chandeliers or sconces or background elements hidden within architecture such as coves, mantles or backlighting details. Visual interest is accomplished by creating layers of light at different visual planes. Unlike the lighting designed for commercial and institutional settings, residential focuses primarily on nighttime illumination, leaving daytime illumination to the interplay of architecture and daylight. Recessed down light locations are intentionally placed and kept to a minimum. They are used to accentuate art, plants, building materials, kitchen counters or other important task areas. To infuse contemporary residential environments with crisp, white light that is easily dimmed, Lightbrigade chooses low voltage halogen as the primary source while traditional homes require the warmth of incandescent. Dimmable low voltage or miniature fluorescent luminaires are hidden in architectural elements. A dimming control system is critical to the success of residential design. While aiding in energy conservation and extending lamp life, intelligent grouping of lights on the control system enables the homeowner to set moods, permitting the creation of dramatic scenes and light variations.

Lightbrigade

Hospitality

Hospitality environments can often be complex, dynamic and demanding. The lighting must attract guests by expressing the level of quality and service being offered. Lighting plays a significant role in way-finding by establishing a hierarchy of light levels that give guests the visual keys to the services they require, such as the front desk, restaurant, bar or spa. Most of the four and five star hotels Lightbrigade designs, are dictated by dated design standards requiring the use of only incandescent lighting in public spaces, despite years of improving technology. As a result, both line and low voltage halogen lighting is the predominant source. Whenever hidden from direct view, Lightbrigade incorporates dimmable fluorescent or cold cathode systems to create uniform washes and reduce energy. LED lighting is starting to appear in specific applications. Dimming systems are used throughout all public spaces to support various functions and extend lamp life. They also represent the main energy conservation method. Hotel designs rarely incorporate daylight, leaning towards a much more intimate environment. A sense of time is maintained with astronomical time clocks that reduce the evening lighting at sunset, conserving energy and quieting the mood of public spaces. At sunrise the cycle is reversed.

1: **InterContinental Hotel Toronto Centre,** lobby, Toronto, ON; Crang & Boake Architects, Richard Dabrus, architect; Michael Mahovlich, photography.

2: **InterContinental Hotel Toronto Centre,** private dining, Toronto, ON; Crang & Boake Architects, Richard Dabrus, architect; Michael Mahovlich, photography.

3: **InterContinental Hotel Toronto Centre,** Azure Bar, Toronto, ON; Crang & Boake Architects, Richard Dabrus, architect; Michael Mahovlich, photography.

Lighting Design Alliance

1234 East Burnett Street
Signal Hill, CA 90755 3510
562.989.3843
562.989.3847 (Fax)
www.lightingdesignalliance.com
info@LightingDesignAlliance.com

Lighting Design Alliance

The Borgata Hotel, Casino & Spa
Atlantic City, New Jersey

5   Targeting a younger and more sophisticated guest than the Atlantic City gaming industry has traditionally claimed, the Borgata Hotel, Casino & Spa has captured market share and the loyalty of affluent customers in the Northeast and beyond with its dazzling display of architecture, interior design and lighting. Lighting Design Alliance, lighting designer of the Borgata, worked closely with other members of a multi-disciplinary design team, including architects Bower Lewis Thrower, Cope Linder Architects, and Marnell Corrao, and interior designers Dougall Design Associates, Laurence Lee Associates, and Inter-Arch Associates, to create unique environments for such facilities as the 135,000-square-foot casino, 70,000-square-foot event space, 50,000-square-foot spa, 2,002 guest rooms, 11 restaurants and 11 retail boutiques. The diversity of activities and spaces is reflected in each of Lighting Design Alliance's solutions. Consider the way lighting complements the registration lobby. At the reception desk, the verticality of the architecture is celebrated day and night with two distinct looks. During the daytime, a wall of drapery is softly illuminated from above for a subdued look. By nightfall, the curtains part to expose a backlit, color-changing water feature wall. Either way, the lighting is part of a powerful message that says: Let's play!

1 - 6: The Borgata Hotel, Casino & Spa, Atlantic City, New Jersey, Bower Lewis Thrower, Cope Linder Architects, Marnell Corrao, architects; Dougall Design Associates, Laurence Lee Associates, Inter-Arch Associates, interior designers; Scott Frances, photographer.

Lighting Design Alliance

1 - 6: Port of Los Angeles, Los Angeles, California, Dyna-lectric, EDAW, Siebert Perkins Design, and Lighting Design Alliance, client/contractor/design team; David Lloyd and Dixi Carrillo/EDAW, photographers.

Port cities are blessed with a precious asset they often industrialize rather than enjoy. However, the Port of Los Angeles, located 20 miles south of downtown in San Pedro Bay, has given its waterfront a more progressive role in community life, maintaining diverse recreational and educational facilities as well as record-setting cargo operations. Los Angeles is one of the world's great commercial ports, encompassing 7,500 acres, 43 miles of waterfront, and 26 cargo terminals that handle over 162 million metric revenue tons of cargo annually. Yet it also offers public spaces that have been designed for sheer pleasure by a client/contractor/design team comprising the Port of Los Angeles,

Dyna-lectric, EDAW, Siebert Perkins Design, and Lighting Design Alliance. The lighting scheme for the meandering paths and palm plazas introduces an architectural presence to the waterfront by day and lends a majestic aura to paving and foliage by night. To make this happen, Lighting Design Alliance has developed light columns for soft, vertical illumination, in-grade LED medallions to uplight palm fronds, a historical reproduction of a beloved 50-year-old "angel light," and a unique "ladder" pole for luminaires and banners inspired by shipping cranes, bringing night life to the Port.

Lighting Design Alliance

Endeavor Talent Agency
Beverly Hills, California

In Hollywood's rarified world of talent agencies, making an architectural statement at the office became de rigeur after CCA recruited the first A-list architect. Now, the Endeavor Talent Agency, representing such television and film celebrities as David E. Kelly (creator of Ally McBeal and The Practice), Aaron Sorkin (creator of The West Wing), Jennifer Garner (star of Alias), members of the Osbourne family, Reese Witherspoon, Jude Law, Martin Scorsese, Matt Damon, and Adam Sandler, has risen to the challenge with a breathtaking new, three-story, 70,000-square-foot office in Beverly Hills, designed by Neil M. Denari Architects as architect and Lighting Design Alliance as lighting designer. The ambitious, award-winning facility, which comprises an 80-seat screening room, pre-function area, conference rooms and remodeled façade as well as private and open offices for some 190 employees, transcends a tight schedule and limited lighting budget to give its previously nondescript 1960s building a

4

chic, edgy, modern look. Careful use of such reliable, off-the-shelf components as T5 fluorescents, compact fluorescents, halogen infrared MR16s and ceramic metal halide sources, all seamlessly integrated with the stunning architecture and graphics, simultaneously reinforces the ethereal mood of the space, limits energy consumption and minimizes maintenance—so cool for so many reasons.

1 - 7: Endeavor Talent Agency, Beverly Hills, California, Neil M. Denari Architects, architect; Benny Chan/Fotoworks, photographer. 2005 IIDA Award of Merit.

Lighting Design Alliance

1 - 5: The Cheesecake Factory, shown in nationwide locations, The Cheesecake Factory, Inc., design firm; The Cheesecake Factory Development Group; photographer, Anthony Gonzalez/A.G.

Evelyn Overton's cheesecake has fed countless people since 1971, when Evelyn and her husband Oscar began selling it from a Los Angeles bakery they named The Cheesecake Factory. Their son David used his mother's confection as the pièce de résistance of a Beverly Hills restaurant he opened in 1978 as The Cheesecake Factory, and today, it remains the pride and joy of one of America's largest restaurant companies, which operates 123 full-service, casual dining restaurants in major metropolitan areas. Interestingly, the restaurant has always been as concerned about its décor as its menu, developing a distinctive environment combining dramatically illuminated murals—created by an employee in 1988—with Egyptian columns, cherry wood and brass trim, and hand-blown lighting fixtures. The current lighting standards, developed by Lighting Design Alliance in collaboration with the company, which designs its restaurants in-house, respects the restaurant's signature style while meeting strict energy standards with maintenance-friendly lamps and luminaires. The design creates multiple layers of light through such strategies as custom-fabricated cold cathode coves and lighting accents, backlit, dimmable T8 mica panels, custom-designed glowing booth ends and coves, uplighted glass dividers, and rhythmic wall accents, enabling customers and food to look their best.

Lighting Design Solutions/
H.H. Angus & Associates Limited

1127 Leslie Street
Toronto, ON, M3C 2J6
Canada
416.443.8200
1.866.741.7282 (Fax)
www.hhangus.com/LDS

Lighting Design Solutions/H.H. Angus & Associates Limited

Terrence Donnelly Centre for Cellular and Biomolecular Research
University of Toronto
Toronto, ON Canada

New facilities designed to satisfy their occupants are helping organizations attract and retain valued personnel: a prime example is the University of Toronto's new, 10-story, 221,120-square-foot Terrence Donnelly Centre for Cellular and Biomolecular Research, lighting design by Lighting Design Solutions. The Centre houses researchers from the Medicine, Pharmacy, Applied Science and Engineering faculties with students and post-doctoral fellows working in state-of-the-art laboratory and teaching facilities. Its functional, flexible and attractive design simultaneously meets the faculty's needs and reaffirms the University's status as a leader in genome research. The role of lighting is visible everywhere. For example, lighting for the wall of the heritage building to the east, and rows of bamboo plants lining the main corridor,

blends daylight and artificial light to promote plant growth while minimizing glare for occupants. The atrium's upper level utilizes spill light from the second floor's suspended fluorescent fixtures. In-ground and color-specific metal halide downlights create an inviting atmosphere for conversation in the main corridor. The colorful glass curtain wall offers the background for outdoor lighting accents. In effect, the Centre and its illumination will light the way for the great minds of the future.

1 - 5: Terrece Donnelly Centre for Cellular and Biomolecular Research,
University of Toronto, Toronto, ON Canada, architectsAlliance/Behnisch, Behnisch & Partner, architects; Tom Arban Photography, photographer.

Lighting Design Solutions/H.H. Angus & Associates Limited

New Clinical Services Building
University Health Network- Toronto General
Toronto, ON Canada

Healthcare facilities are evolving rapidly as funding models change, technology drives innovation and the environment itself becomes part of the healing process. Lighting Design Solutions leverages over 60 years of lighting design experience to enrich the "healing environment" through illumination. The firm's insights into the technical and experiential aspects of "brightening" the healthcare experience are demonstrated in its engineering services for four new buildings at the 353-bed campus of Toronto General Hospital. For the 12-story, 600,000-square-foot new Clinical Services Building, the challenge was to illuminate an environment that combines the latest medical technologies with a welcoming atmosphere conducive to patient recovery. Consider the Patient Court, a four-story atrium offering respite, hope and inspiration, where ceiling-mounted, color-corrected metal halide luminaires

simulate natural light. Lighting is available for every procedure and scenario in 22 state-of-the-art operating rooms. Patient rooms incorporate multi-purpose luminaires with individual patient controls and secondary lighting systems to balance a home-like feeling with clinical requirements. The facility makes an impression, whether the viewer is simply passing the campus on the street or navigating the halls of the buildings. LDS/HHA researched the user requirements and actively participated in the design of the project with the architect in order to deliver thoughtful and innovative lighting solutions.

1 - 5: New Clinical Services Building, Toronto General Hospital, Toronto, ON Canada, HOK Canada, architect; David Whitaker & Ben Rahn, photographers.

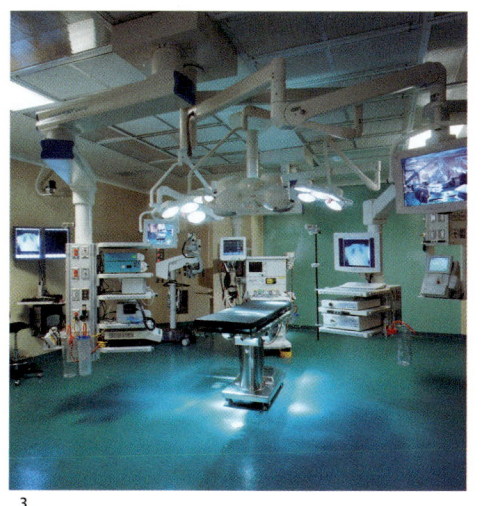

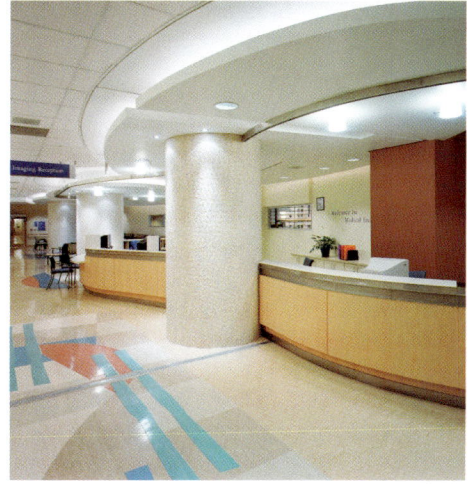

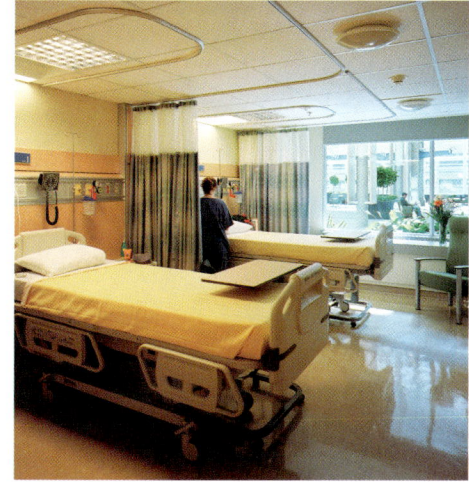

3

4

5

Lighting Design Solutions/H.H. Angus & Associates Limited

Sheraton Centre Toronto
Starwood Hotels & Resorts Worldwide, Inc.
Toronto, ON Canada

1 - 5: **Sheraton Centre Toronto,** Toronto, ON Canada,
Sievenpiper Associates Inc., architect; Garry Kan, photographer.

Hospitality and restaurant operators know physical space is as critical as service for repeat business. For this reason, Lighting Design Solutions works closely with architects, interior designers and image consultants to produce memorable guest experiences. In the remodeling of the 1,377-room Sheraton Centre Toronto, Lighting Design Solutions helped effect a sweeping transformation. The utilitarian motor court and lobby of 1967 have re-emerged as a porte cochere and living room worthy of important guests. The motor court's asphalt and concrete have yielded to an Arrival Court featuring an estate garden, limestone-clad main entrance with gas-lit luminaires, color-corrected metal halide downlights and wall sconces that simulate daylight by increasing the light level to 100 footcandles. Inside, the new, residential-style lobby of wood and leather employs varied lighting techniques to produce an atmosphere for relaxing and socializing, including specially designed chandeliers with two-color LED candelabra lamps, compact fluorescents and PAR 38 lamps, aided by wall sconces, table lamps and a dimming system. Similar changes in the remodeled ballroom and conference rooms ensure that the Sheraton Centre Toronto will effectively turn new guests into repeat customers.

Lighting Design Solutions/H.H. Angus & Associates Limited

TD Securities - Investment Banking
Toronto Dominion Bank Tower
Toronto, ON Canada

Corporate spaces that require quality lighting depend on design collaboration among architects, interior designers, furniture planners and lighting designers. Having honed its skills serving Fortune 500 companies, Lighting Design Solutions excels in communicating with clients and consultants, in order to illuminate spaces that perform to their full potential and project the corporate vision. The benefits can be seen in the high-profile commercial reception and conference areas for TD Securities' 40,000-square-foot investment banking office at Toronto Dominion Bank Tower. A dual approach to lighting in the reception area gives the space multi-functional capability by using compact fluorescent downlights for general illumination and low-voltage MR16 wall sconces for accent lighting, both controlled by a complex dimming system. The video conference room lighting balances strict AV constraints for projection and image capture with users' needs for vertical and horizontal illumination, using dimmable compact fluorescent downlights over the table, adjustable, low-voltage MR16 downlights directed towards the walls, and automated window shades. By taking advantage of changing AV and lighting equipment technologies, Lighting Design Solutions designs for the latest developments and for the future.

1 - 3: **TD Securities,** Investment Banking, Toronto, ON Canada, HOK Canada, interior designer; Patrick Kennedy, photographer.

The Lighting Practice, Inc.

128 Chestnut Street
Suite 401
Philadelphia, PA 19106
215.238.1644
215.238.1674 (Fax)
www.thelightingpractice.com

The Lighting Practice, Inc.

Could one of the nation's best-established and most successful shopping centers possibly be made bigger and better? At Houston's Galleria Mall, America's fifth largest retail center with 2.4 million square feet, the answer is definitely yes. The Lighting Practice recently participated in a 229,000-square-foot renovation and expansion of the original 1970 mall and 1980 addition with Cooper Carry Architects, covering three retail levels, the Ice Rink, the Food Court, department store courts, and the Fountain Court, celebrating and embellishing the Galleria's high-fashion elegance. The lighting has been sensitively integrated with the architecture, employing such means as multiple-lamp downlights, backlighted translucent panels, concealed uplights, and custom luminaires for general and accent lighting; point-source lighting to reflect off polished architectural finishes and add patina to public areas; PAR lamps in the fountain base, up/down sconces on the columns, and concealed

luminaires in the coves at Fountain Court; pendant lighting and theatrical ellipsoidal projects in the department store courts; and both decorative hanging fixtures and adjustable ceiling illumination in the Food Court. In granting an Award of Merit in 2004 from the International Association of Lighting Designers, jurors noted, "The Galleria's lighting really serves the purpose of the space—high-end shopping."

1 - 4: **Galleria Mall,** Houston, Texas, Cooper Carry Architects, architect; Gabriel Benzur, photographer.

The Lighting Practice, Inc.

Prime Outlets San Marcos

The assignment: Transform an already successful shopping center on Interstate 35 in San Marcos, Texas to distinguish it from its competition directly across the street, and increase its appeal to existing and new customers from Austin to the north and San Antonio to the south. Architect Carter & Burgess teamed with The Lighting Practice to design the 850,000-square-foot renovation and expansion of the 130-store Prime Outlets San Marcos, one of 27 upscale Prime Outlets malls in 18 states, changing a Spanish Colonial setting into a Venetian one. Consequently, Prime Outlets San Marcos features such Venetian motifs as a clock tower, campanile, covered colonnaded walkway, and canal with gondolas and footbridges. Lighting enhances the center at multiple levels. While decorative post lights and wall brackets resembling the pedestrian lights in St. Mark's Square provide sidewalk illumination, parking lot floodlighting imparts a soft wash on buildings, color-changing LED wall washers animate the façade of the central Nieman Marcus building and its clock tower, and special lighting for rooftops and towers makes everything visible from surrounding roadways, a critical detail that ensures that customers won't miss the chance to shop at Prime Outlets San Marcos and visit "Venice" at the same time.

1 - 2: Prime Outlets San Marcos, San Marcos, Texas, Carter & Burgess, architect; J. Brough Schamp, photographer.

The Lighting Practice, Inc.

Children's Hospital of Philadelphia

For thousands of anxious patients, parents and staff who use "I-95," the nickname for a newly remodeled corridor at the Children's Hospital of Philadelphia that serves as the main internal connector between the hospital's ambulatory, parking and inpatient facilities, moving along the 150-foot long, 2,000-square-foot passage is an unexpected delight. The elongated space, designed by Karlsberger as architect with The Lighting Practice as lighting designer, reflects the simple, visually soothing and uplifting environment sought by the Hospital to inspire families and their sick children. The design team's low-tech solution for I-95 is based on backlighted colored images of recovered patients mounted on graphic panels that are tightly spaced for maximum visual impact. To simplify replacement of the images and facilitate lighting maintenance, graphic panels are customized with removable side rails and illuminated with readily available T8 fluorescent lamps. There's even a surprise at the corridor entry. Automated gobo projectors produce moving patterns of stars and moons on the floor via two recessed luminaires fitted with dichroic color filters and a ceramic metal halide lamp, all easily serviced through ceiling trim. Children forget where they are—at least momentarily—to chase the celestial bodies that the low-cost and easily updated design makes possible.

1: **Children's Hospital of Philadelphia,** I-95 Corridor, Philadelphia, Pennsylvania, Karlsberger, architect; Barry Halkin, photographer.

The Lighting Practice, Inc.

Benjamin Franklin Parkway

Philadelphia's Benjamin Franklin Parkway is revealed by day as one of the city's most majestic boulevards. Extending one mile from City Hall to the Philadelphia Museum of Art and lined with museums, public art and groves of trees, it remains true to the original plan by architects Paul P. Cret and Jacques Greber, designer of the Parkway's Rodin Museum. Now, thanks to a relighting program, designed by Cope Linder Architects with The Lighting Practice, exterior lighting provides nightly illumination for seven historic, Greek Revival-style building façades and 13 works of sculpture by such artists as Calder, Lipchitz and Rodin. A prime goal was to reveal the original intent of each architect and artist in color and form. In a meticulous installation of discretely placed equipment, including five metal halide lamp types and seven pole-mounted luminaire types, light is aimed to bring visual depth to architectural and sculptural details while limiting glare and light trespass onto the roadway. Yet the new lighting design, winner of an Illumination Design Award from the Philadelphia Section of the Illuminating Engineering Society, remains natural in appearance, because the lighting generally beams down from sources concealed among the trees, reprising the grandeur of daylight after sunset.

1 - 5: **Benjamin Franklin Parkway,** Façade and Sculpture Lighting, Philadelphia, Pennsylvania, Cope Linder Architects, architect; Tom Crane, photographer.

The Lighting Practice, Inc.

International Management Consulting Firm

A sophisticated lighting design conceived to give a cool, clean, contemporary look to the new Philadelphia headquarters of a major international consulting firm is so skillfully integrated into the one-story, 24,000-square-foot interior at the Cira Centre in Center City, designed by Ballinger as architect with The Lighting Practice as lighting designer, that it calls no attention to itself. Yet its presence is felt in numerous ways throughout the reception and waiting areas, private offices, administrative spaces, elevator lobby, corridors and conference rooms. Recessed and wall-mounted light fixtures predominate the installation, reinforcing the space's affinity with the building's contemporary architecture and maximizing the floor's views of the Philadelphia skyline. Frosted glass walls are accentuated by indirect fluorescent lighting in conference rooms and perimeter offices. The concept of glowing planes is extended through luminous panel fluorescent uplights suspended in the multi-purpose room's coffers and in the café's wall sconces. Fluorescent coves between ceiling planes emphasize the interplay of lines and edges in the architecture. Square compact fluorescent downlights and wall washers appear as luminous apertures in the ceiling plane. The lighting thus compliments a sleek, modern interior where everything else strives towards the same efficiency, comfort and style.

1 - 3: International Management Consulting Firm, Philadelphia, Pennsylvania, Ballinger, architect; Chun Lai, photographer.

The Lighting Practice, Inc.

Johnson & Johnson, Consumer Products Worldwide

Johnson & Johnson's former diaper manufacturing factory in Skillman, New Jersey seems an unlikely site for a bright, spacious and inviting office building, research center and pilot plant—until you see its recent, one-level, 450,000-square-foot total renovation, designed by Ballinger and The Lighting Practice. To transform the vast, 475-foot by 950-foot expanse into the headquarters for Johnson & Johnson's Consumer Products Worldwide, despite a modest budget and a requirement for low maintenance, the primary architectural and lighting solutions combine natural light with electric illumination. A key factor in the makeover was the opening of a large, elliptical skylight, creating a 28-foot-high, daylight-filled atrium that functions as the new facility's geographic center and gathering place. T8 fluorescent lamps, metal halide lamps, and metal halide PAR lamps are strategically positioned in the atrium to supplement daylight as needed. Elsewhere, the staff's various tasks are lighted with equal attention to detail through standard luminaires equipped with fluorescent and metal halide lamps that also combine their output with available daylight. Consequently, the lighting design, granted an International Illumination Design Award Of Merit by the Mid-Atlantic Region of the Illuminating Engineering Society, helps Johnson & Johnson see what's important at all times.

The Lighting Practice, Inc.

Clay Center for the Arts & Sciences

Lighting acts like a performer in the new, four-story, 240,000-square-foot Clay Center for the Arts & Sciences, in Charleston, West Virginia. Designed by Kise Straw Kolodner and Gates Calloway Moore & West as associated architects and The Lighting Practice as lighting designer, the Clay Center houses the 1,883-seat Maier Foundations Concert Hall, two-level Juliet Museum of Art, and two-level Avampato Science Museum. Though lighting requirements change for each institution, the lighting design, which received an Illumination Design Award from the Philadelphia Section of the Illuminating Engineering Society, shifts gears effortlessly. For example, halogen PAR sources provide uplighting, downlighting and wallwashing in the Performing Arts Lobby. In the Maier Foundations Concert Hall, recessed halogen PARs and monopoint luminaires on catwalks light the seating, LED strips in stair risers and halogens in seating fascias define aisles, and optical fibers, illuminated by ceramic metal halide lamps, provide edge-lighting on balcony fascias. Halogen PARs on movable tracks light exhibits in the Avampato Science Museum. Exhibits in the Juliet Museum of Art, by contrast, use halogen luminaires on recessed tracks inside ceiling coffers, producing a soft visual environment distinct from the Center's other venues. Wherever attendees go, the Clay Center lights the way accordingly.

1 - 3: Clay Center for the Arts & Sciences, Charleston, West Virginia, Kise Straw Kolodner and Gates Calloway Moore & West, associated architects; James West, photographer.

LIGHTVISION, LLC

1213 South Ogden Drive
Los Angeles, CA 90019
323.932.0700
323.571.0940 (Fax)
www.lightvision.com

LIGHTVISION, LLC

Entertainment/Retail

Entertainment and retail environments challenge us to create places that are scintillating, compelling people to visit, eat, shop, and ultimately arrive for a great experience. **LIGHT**VISION explores new ways to bring a fresh and inspirational approach to these projects. When we are successful, customers have a great time, spend millions of dollars, and return to do it again. Options abound when lighting a performing arts center, mall, night club, or park. The owner, architect, landscape architect, interior designer, and lighting designer need to team up to produce a space that is extraordinary and practical. Some of the items we look to light in a playful, dramatic, and even classical way include art, textures, plants, signs, structures, architectural and water features. Our goal is for a highly successful project and profitable, happy owner.

1: **California Polytechnic University,** Performing Arts Center, San Luis Obispo, California, Warnecke/DMJM, architect; Allan Leibow, photographer.

2: **Doral Saturnia,** Miami, Florida, Jung/Brannen Associates, architect; Tom Lee Ltd., interior designer; George Cott, photographer.

3: **Tsunami Night Club,** Maui, Hawaii, Chapman Desai Sakata, Inc. architect, Barry Design Associates, interior design; Jaime Ardiles-Arce, photographer.

4: **Paramount Pictures Office Building,** Hollywood, California, Gensler, architect; Hedrich Blessing, photographer.

5: **Paramount Theater,** Hollywood, California, Gensler, architect; Hedrich Blessing, photographer.

6: **460 N. Canon,** Beverly Hills, California, Rockefeller/Hricak architects; David Glome, photographer.

LIGHTVISION, LLC

Office environment lighting should provide both a lighting source and a comfortable, pleasing experience. Hours spent at work rival those at home, and we feel that the relaxed, happy employee will perform better, resulting in fewer mistakes and injuries. Spaces where veiling reflections and glare are minimized to allow for clarity and reduced fatigue for the worker. Optimum office lighting is not uniform, as even light throughout can be tedious. Having dark and light areas for eyes to focus is important. Daylight, being both natural and offering the best color, is invaluable, as it can be used with filtering devices such as window shades and louvers. It creates an atmosphere that lifts morale and improves people's performance. Controls and sensors at windows help reduce energy consumption and cost.

1: Altoon + Porter offices, Los Angeles, California, Altoon + Porter, architect; Fred Licht Photos, photographer.

2: 201 Santa Monica, Santa Monica, California, Dianna Wong Architcture & Design, architect; Douglas Emmet, owner; Wayne Thom, photographer.

3: Maguire Partners, Headquarters, Los Angeles, California, CNI Design, interior designer; Benny Chan Fotoworks, photographer.

4: Paramount Pictures Office Building, Hollywood California, Gensler, architect, Hedrich Blessing, photographer.

Lighting for temples and churches should support the powerful, spiritual experience one has at religious facilities. Providing focused light on key elements such as a speaker, bride and groom, religious artifacts, art, and donor walls, etc., gives importance to the people and objects. Areas in between the features can remain darker, setting up a composition and hierarchy in prime locations, supplying drama and intimacy. Decorative fixtures create a human scale and bring art and detail to the sanctuary, lobbies, and classrooms. Stained and colored glass are backlit at night with carefully placed luminaires. By day the sun projects rich colors and patterns through these same windows onto the sanctuary below. A properly designed building bounces light off deep skylight wells or light shelves, spreading and softening the natural light. Using daylight effectively, simply put, conserves energy.

1: **Peoples Church,** Fresno, California, Marette Denninger, Darrell Howe & Associates, architect.

2: **Wailea Chapel,** Maui, Hawaii, Chapman Desai Sakata, Inc. architect; Barry Design Associates, Interior Designer; Jaime Ardiles-Arce, photographer.

3: **Temple Solel,** Encinitas, California, Goldman, Firth, Rossi Architects, architect; Wayne Thom, photographer.

LIGHTVISION, LLC

As a homeowner feels his or her environment is an oasis of warmth, comfort, and intimacy, so should a hotel guest. Hotels and residences share many lighting challenges despite the larger scale and complexity of hotels, which include restaurants, ballrooms, and retail shops. **LIGHT**VISION pursues similar approaches for both environments; concealing fixtures to reveal architectural details, projecting pools of light on furniture, art and plants, for inviting focal areas; designing slots in ceilings to graze light on walls; and using decorative fixtures for a warm, soft light. Color is used selectively to evoke emotion, such as a serene reddish light in a restaurant that is "cut" with a pure white halogen source to feature tables and art. For homes and hotels, filtered and direct daylight should flood the interiors for a bright and natural feel, along with the appropriate window treatments and controls. To conserve energy while providing drama and intimacy, **LIGHT**VISION honors a philosophy defined by the late Lesley Wheel, the first female architectural lighting designer; "Put light only where it is needed."

1: **Ritz Carlton,** San Francisco, California, Kajima Associates, architect; John Sutton, photographer.

2: **Ehrlich Residence,** Santa Monica, California, John Friedman Alice Kimm Architects; Benny Chan Fotoworks, photographer.

3: **Shilla Hotel,** Lobby Lounge, Seoul, Korea, Remedios Siembieda Associates, interior designer.

4: **University of Southern California,** Borvard Hall, WWCOT, architect.

5: **Kahala Mandarin,** Honolulo, Hawaii, KSLW Architects, architect; Hirsch Bedner Associates, interior designer.

6: **Watermark Hotel,** San Antonio, Texas, HKS Architects, architect; Karen Rogers/Tamara Sypult, Hirsch Bedner Associates, interior designer; Michael Wilson, photographer.

7: **ANA Hotel,** San Francisco, California, Callison Partnership, architect; Barry Design Associates, interior designers; John Sutton, photographer.

1 - 2: Large scale condominium complex, Los Angeles, California, Yuki Anzai, renderer.

At night, all features from trees and paths to buildings and structures are primarily visible using electric light; everything else becomes dark. **LIGHT**VISION's philosophy is to deliver lighting that feels natural, provides safety, and is inviting. Intimate areas can be moonlit from trees, while art, feature trees and plants, and fountains become focal points. Due to increased contrast outdoors, fixtures should have maximum shielding to minimize glare. Buildings and structures serve as the backdrop in streets and cities and are lit in a variety of

ways, depending on the architecture. Some options for lighting a contemporary building include fluorescent or LED light washes and slowly changing, colored points of light; while a historic building may be softly lit with HPS. From an airplane, the city light that you see at night is wasted because it is not achieving its desired target. **LIGHT**VISION aims to solve such problems by using efficient and sophisticated optics for the benefit of the environment.

Luminae Souter Associates, LLC

504 Roosevelt Way
San Francisco, CA 94114
415.863.8800
415.863.8808 (Fax)
www.luminae-souter.com

Luminae Souter Associates, LLC

Westin Palo Alto
Palo Alto, California

Business people choose to register at the Westin Palo Alto, in Palo Alto, California, to enjoy direct access to Stanford University and the local entrepreneurs, venture capitalists, scientists and engineers who make Silicon Valley a hotbed of technological innovation and exponential wealth. Consequently, the new, 184-room hotel, designed by Sandy & Babcock, Inc., architect, Jennifer Puhalla and Ron Aguila/Tom & Aguila, interior designer, and Luminae Souter Associates, LLC, lighting designer, offers guests a California casual boutique-style oasis for winding down and relaxing between high-powered meetings. Guestrooms, business center, meeting rooms, restaurant, lounge and gym all contribute to the inviting, residential ambiance through Mediterranean-style architecture, lush gardens, calming water features and warm lighting. The several lamp types used, for example, exhibit harmonious color temperatures in the warm 2700-3000K range. High color rendering, energy-efficient fluorescent lighting prevails wherever possible, supplemented by low-voltage xenon and halogen sources. Lighting also reinforces the themes that characterize the hotel's Garden Courts. At the Court of the Sun and Moon, shown here, uplighting on decorative pots conveys the feeling of a setting sun as wall-mounted sconces mimic a lunar eclipse—projecting far-reaching images that succinctly capture the high-tech spirit of the Valley.

1 - 5: Westin Palo Alto, Palo Alto, California, Sandy & Babcock, Inc., architect; Jennifer Puhalla and Ron Aguila/ Tom & Aguila, interior designer; John Sutton, photographer. IES IIDA National Award of Merit.

Luminae Souter Associates, LLC

1 - 5: Private Residence, San Francisco, California, Form 4 Architecture, architect; JD Peterson, photographer. First Place/Residential, 2005 National Lighting Competition SOURCE Award.

The lighting design that dramatizes the architecture of a new San Francisco residence fulfills an unusual technical requirement. It compensates for high daylight contrasts while capturing and redistributing daylight—inside a home that happens to be a 2,000-square-foot penthouse with northeast views atop a high-rise structure. However, the residence, designed by Form 4 Architecture, architect, and Luminae Souter Associates, LLC, lighting designer, is as impressive as its surroundings. Early collaboration between architect and lighting designer has produced a scheme with translucent panels, internal fenestration and extensive built-in lighting. Not surprisingly, the lighting's nuances rely on an array of sophisticated devices.

Besides a lighting control system that accommodates day and nighttime scenes with maximum flexibility, energy conservation and convenience, providing programmed pre-sets to meet the client's lifestyle and needs, automated nightlights for client and guests, and conveniently located keypads, there are photocells and occupancy sensors that automate lighting, and lighting that complements an ambitious ceiling design. While a 24V xenon strip adapts to the ceiling's various curves, 12V halogen MR-16 lamps illuminate the lower ceiling areas, incorporating various downlights where needed. In the end, the ceiling and everything below it looks as splendid to the client as the spectacle outdoors.

Luminae Souter Associates, LLC

Netflix
Headquarters
Los Gatos, California

1 - 4: Netflix, , Los Gatos, California, Form 4 Architecture, architect; John Sutton, photographer.

Operating the world's largest online DVD movie rental service, providing 5.7 million members access to 65,000 titles, Netflix has grown steadily since 1999 by giving members what they want. Its attention to both general concept and operational detail shows up in its new, three-story, 80,000-square-foot headquarters in Los Gatos, California, designed by Form 4 Architecture, architect, and Luminae Souter Associates, LLC, lighting designer. The contemporary facility, part of a mixed-use development and transit hub, gives employees various stimulating workplace environments that are defined by changes in carpet, walls and ceilings, and connected with a fluid circulation plan. The

lighting design is carefully tailored to each space. Softly diffused high color rendering 3000K color temperature fluorescent lighting is integrated with curved walls and ceilings to accentuate graceful curves in connecting corridors and illuminate pathways. High efficiency T5 fluorescent lamps are suspended at angles in harmony with the curved soffits in open ceiling areas, using perforated metal shields clipped onto lamps to mitigate glare. Compact fluorescent downlights with high efficiency reflectors provide soft general illumination to establish a fresh, uncluttered corporate image in the main lobby, at the same time sparkling accents from halogen sources in decorative translucent pendants

Luminae Souter Associates, LLC

Netflix
Headquarters
Los Gatos, California

and frosted glass-covered recessed downlights introduce specific focal points and visual interest. By contrast, the unconventional theater used as a video presentation space and speaker's forum employs a diverse assortment of light sources and fixtures for maximum flexibility. Miniature LED lights illuminate the steps when theater lights are flow, adjustable PAR38 halogen spots with barn door shutters highlight the stage area, and general lighting comes from two sources: halogen pendants mounted between acoustic ceiling panels, projecting soft dramatic pools of downlight when a minimum amount of general light is required, and dimmable T5 fluorescent strip lights with perforated back shields for higher light levels. Accents are furnished through decorative sconces and wall washers, and a sophisticated, multiple-scene lighting system lets users set up pre-set combinations of functions, including the raising and lowering of the screen and window shades. Equipped with such thoughtful design features, Netflix's employees could be as satisfied as its customers.

PETERS & MYER
The Lighting Design Studio of O'MAHONY & MYER

4340 Redwood Hwy
Suite 245
San Rafael, CA 94903
415.492.0420
415.479.9662 (Fax)
www.ommconsulting.com

PETERS & MYER
The Lighting Design Studio of O'MAHONY & MYER

In the days after a disastrous fire destroyed St. Matthew's Episcopal Church along with 86 homes in Pacific Palisades, California, the Parish decided to transform the tragedy into an opportunity to unite the church community in the act of building anew. What made this award-winning project more than a conventional exercise was the use of a radical participatory design method involving all interested parties—architects, consultants, church elders, lay congregation representatives and members, and clergy—in openly conducted design charettes. The renowned architect Charles Moore and his firm, Moore Ruble Yudell, joined forces with long-time collaborator, Richard Peters, founding principal of Peters & Myer, and the church community to address all critical areas of the new church. The proposed conceptual architectural/lighting design easily achieved the two-thirds vote of the Parish, as required for approval to

St. Matthew's Episcopal Church
Pacific Palisades, California

proceed. Nothing was withheld from the completed installation, including the magnificent, custom-designed decorative pendant lighting fixtures, which were modeled at full scale and installed in the main worship hall, as part of an architectural mock-up, assembled for client group evaluations. The result of this uncommon effort was an exceptional lighting design, integrating custom-designed decorative lighting fixtures with natural daylighting introduced at key architectural locations. The full-scale mock-up so inspired church members that the additional funds to cover the cost for the custom luminaries were effortlessly raised in record time.

1 - 5: St. Matthew's Episcopal Church, Pacific Palisades, California, Charles Moore, Moore Ruble Yudell, architect; Richard Peters, Peters & Myer, lighting designer; Timothy Hursley, photographer.

2

3

4

5

PETERS & MYER
The Lighting Design Studio of O'MAHONY & MYER

Christopher B. Smith Rafael Film Center
San Rafael, California

Superbly revived by the Northern California Film Institute after a storied history marked by such moments as its 1918 opening as a first-run movie house, 1926 expansion, 1937 fire, and 1938 remodeling in the Art Moderne style, the Christopher B. Smith Rafael Film Center, in San Rafael, California now functions as a state-of-the-art 600-seat triplex movie theater for art and foreign films, as well as a major venue for the Film Institute's annual Mill Valley Film Festival and associated fundraising events. San Francisco architect Mark Cavagnero retained O'Mahony & Myer / Peters & Myer (who provided a portion of their services pro bono) for the extensive electrical engineering and lighting design work, including: complete restoration of the original façade and marquis, ticket booth, lobby and main theater, plus integration and remodel of an adjacent building to accommodate a new screening room, banquet room, staff offices, meeting rooms and an art gallery. The sophisticated lighting design retained the original art deco chandeliers and sconces (refurbished and optically modernized), while integrating new energy-efficient light fixtures and computer controls throughout. The renovated main theater, as well as the two new film theaters, were engineered for the screening of all media formats, including traditional film, digital HD broadcast and DVD, with THX certified audio systems (with components and the services of his THX Division engineering design staff donated by George Lucas). The auditorium-style lighting and dimming provisions in the renovated main theater and precedes allow it to serve as the Institute's primary venue for fundraising events.

1

2

3

4

5

1 - 7: Christopher B. Smith Rafael Film Center (formerly the Rafael Theater),
San Rafael, California, Mark Cavagnero, architect; O'Mahony & Myer, electrical engineer; Peters & Myer, lighting designer; Sharon Risedorph, photographer.

PETERS & MYER
The Lighting Design Studio of O'MAHONY & MYER

Dublin Library
Dublin, California

One of the more intriguing reasons why the new, single-story, 30,000-square-foot Dublin Library, in Dublin, California, designed by BSA Architects, architect, Peters & Myer, lighting designer, and O'Mahony & Myer, electrical engineer, is so attractive and efficient is that its state-of-the-art illumination systems simultaneously provide functional lighting for all tasks and effective lighting of the architectural features. From the metal halide pole fixtures leading from the Civic Center Campus parking lot to the building and the in-grade metal halide fixtures illuminating Robert Ellison's stylized "Know Way" columns at the entry, to the individually tailored solutions inside, the lighting scheme addresses the wishes of architects and librarians while respecting the boundaries set by the construction budget and California's Title 24 energy standards.

The entry rotunda, for example, welcomes visitors to a grand space lighted by a large, custom, circular, indirect/direct pendant fixture and fluorescent cove. The main reading room employs a task/ambient approach with large diameter decorative fluorescent pendants. And the stepped ceiling over the storytime area in the children's reading space glows with concentric cove lighting to reinforce the sense of a public forum where reading aloud is a universal pleasure.

1 - 5: **Dublin Public Library,** Dublin, California, BSA Architects, architect; O'Mahony & Myer, electrical engineer; Peters & Myer, lighting designer; Douglas A. Salin (images 2, 4 & 5) and Tom Rider (images 1 & 3), photographers.

PETERS & MYER
The Lighting Design Studio of O'MAHONY & MYER

St. Francis Winery
Kenwood, California

Big, bold, full-bodied wines have been produced by St. Francis Winery & Vineyards, in Kenwood, California, in a modern Winery facility since 1999. Now, oenophiles can savor St. Francis wines in a new, 7,500-square-foot Visitors Center & Tasting Room, designed in the California Mission style by Hall & Bartley, architect of the existing 120,000-square-foot Winery and 10,000-square-foot Administration Building, and Peters & Myer, lighting designer for the entire complex. The lighting design approach mirrors each activity: industrial lighting in the Winery, upscale commercial lighting in the Administration Building, and outdoor, decorative and concealed lighting for the landscaping, architecture and interior design of the Visitors Center & Tasting Room. Naturally, the aesthetics of the fixtures in the Visitors Center & Tasting Room parallel the architectural elements in their forms, finishes and colors, even as they stress efficiency, long-life and easy maintenance. Thus, highly decorative, low-wattage incandescent chandeliers, pendants and sconces are prominently installed in the public tasting room, private reserve tasting room, retail store and special event dining facility, accompanied by recessed compact fluorescent downlights, wall-washing fixtures, and indirect compact fluorescent ambient systems, with concealed, low voltage incandescent track lighting in the tasting rooms and retail store—a wine lover's paradise in lights.

176

SBLD Studio

132 West 36th Street
New York, NY 10018
212.391.4230
212.391.4231 (Fax)
www.sbldstudio.com

SBLD Studio

Public Spaces

What distinguishes public spaces from other environments? In public building projects ranging from contemporary to neo-classical styles, and from new construction to adaptive re-use of landmark buildings, SBLD Studio uses lighting to support the activities they host and the civic values they symbolize. To do this effectively, SBLD Studio employs numerous strategies. For example, in the Mary & Charles Babcock Wing of the Reynolda House Museum of American Art, a 30,000-square-foot addition to an existing 1912 house that now serves as a museum, originally designed by Charles Barton Keen, in Winston-Salem, North Carolina, and Schermerhorn Symphony Hall, a new, neo-classical-style, four-story, 197,000-square-foot concert hall in Nashville, Tennessee, both daylight and electric lighting elements are sensitively integrated within the architectural envelope. There are also special opportunities for distinctive features, such as the design of iconic custom fixtures at Schermerhorn Symphony Hall, and the rehabilitation of historic fixtures to reinforce the Art Deco style of the Frist Center for the Visual Arts, a 100,000-square-foot conversion of a landmark Post Office Building into a new venue for fine art, also in Nashville. In any event, SBLD Studio has the in-house capabilities to take a public space assignment from conceptual ideas to implementation.

1, 3: Schermerhorn Symphony Hall, Nashville, Tennessee, David M. Schwarz/Architectural Services, Inc., Earl Swensson Associates, Inc., Hastings Architecture Associates, LLC, architects; ©Attila Uysal/SBLD Studio, photographer.

2, 4: Frist Center for the Visual Arts, Nashville, Tennessee, Tuck Hinton Architects, architect; Tim Hursley—The Arkansas Office, photographer.

5: Reynolda House Museum of American Art, Mary & Charles Babcock Wing, Winston-Salem, North Carolina, Beyer Blinder Belle, architect; ©Elliot Kaufman, photographer.

1

2

3

4

5

SBLD Studio

A business-like attitude towards commercial buildings in today's competitive marketplace often demands more than just basic lighting. Consider the commercial building projects designed by SBLD Studio, which span the spectrum from single-tenant corporate headquarters to developer-sponsored speculative buildings, covering both urban and suburban locations and involving interior as well as exterior areas. Inspired by architectural concepts and materials, SBLD Studio provides lighting design services that create inspiring corporate images and strong curb appeal through dramatic lighting effects. Yet lighting solutions with visual impact are good business for our clients, because we always balance aesthetics with their needs and priorities for functionality, sustainability, maintenance and budget. Thus, an investment in quality lighting yields exceptional returns for such projects as Brooks/World Com headquarters, a dramatic, five-story, 180,000-square-foot structure comprising two buildings linked by nine bridges through a triangular atrium with eight waterfalls, in St. Louis, Missouri; Ayava Communications headquarters, a four-story, 240,000-square-foot conversion of an existing office park building, encompassing the exterior and drop-off area in addition to the interior, to become a coolly modern corporate home office, in Basking Ridge, New Jersey; and 350 Madison Avenue, a renovation of an existing office building lobby, in New York, New York.

1: **Brooks/World Com headquarters,** St. Louis, Missouri, Tuck Hinton Architects, architect; ©Sam Fentress, photographer.

2: **350 Madison Avenue,** New York, New York, Skidmore, Owings & Merrill, architect; ©Eduard Hueber, Archphoto, photographer.

3: **Ayava Communications,** Basking Ridge, New Jersey, Fox & Fowle, architect; SPACE, interior designer; ©Andrew Gordon, photographer.

1

2

3

SBLD Studio

1, 2: Changi Airport, Airport Rail Station, Singapore, Skidmore, Owings & Merrill, architect; ©Tim Griffith, photographer.

3: JFK International Airport, Arrivals Terminal 4, Jamaica, New York, Skidmore, Owings & Merrill, architect; ©Jeff Goldberg/ESTO Photographics, photographer.

Large as the Airbus 380 "super jumbo" airliner is, its proportions are easily surpassed by many of today's transportation facilities, which can be enormous. Designing illumination for these structures requires a creative, broad-brush stroke. The approach certainly works for the new, 1.5 million-square-foot JFK International Arrivals Terminal, in Jamaica, New York, a building that replaces a 1957 predecessor on the same, 165-acre site, and dramatically improves passenger service through separate levels for departures and arrivals, consolidated ticketing and baggage operations, improved customer facilities, duty-free and retail shops, restaurants and other food services. SBLD Studio designed an indirect HID lighting system that provides a soft glow of ambient light in the 50-foot-high ticketing hall, using fixtures hidden above the ticketing kiosks to make the ceiling appear weightless. For the seemingly infinite glass bridge inside a tunnel at Changi Airport's metrorail station, in Singapore, SBLD Studio created a soft wash of light that gives passengers an image of lightness and infinity despite the facility's subterranean location. The space thus becomes a positive experience for people coming and going from the connection bridge and tunnel to the station's rail platform, atria, mezzanine and landscape/fountain garden—and a reminder of how exciting travel can be.

SBLD Studio

Wielding light almost as an artist handles a brush, SBLD Studio creates a unique identity and feel for each corporate project, serving businesses that run the gamut from law firms and financial institutions to media and advertising agencies. The use of lighting design by SBLD Studio as a medium to transform typical workspaces into dynamic, user-friendly environments can be effective on spaces as small as single-floor facilities for young, up-and-coming firms or as large as corporate headquarters for industry giants. For projects requiring more than standard lighting design services, SBLD Studio offers daylighting analysis and assistance with LEED and energy codes that can produce sophisticated, state-of-the-art lighting installations. How convincing the effects can be is demonstrated by such SBLD Studio projects as General Dynamics, a 134,000-square-foot corporate headquarters, in Fairview, Virginia; Kirkpatrick & Lockhart, an 81,000-square-foot law office, in New York, New York; Towers Perrin, an professional services consultant's office, in Stamford, Connecticut; Diageo, a 300,000-square-foot North American

headquarters for the worldwide distributor of premium spirits, in Norwalk, Connecticut; Brown Rudnick Berlack Israels LLP, a 44,000-square-foot law office, in New York, New York; and Lehman-Smith + McLeish, an architect's office, in Washington, D.C.

1: **Lehman-Smith + McLeish,** Washington, D.C., Lehman-Smith + McLeish, architect; ©Eric Laignel, photographer.

2: **Towers Perrin,** Stamford, Connecticut, Perkins & Will, architect; ©Mike Houlihan/Hedrich Blessing, photographer.

3: **Kirkpatrick & Lockhart,** New York, New York, Lehman-Smith & McLeish, architect; ©Jon Miller/Hedrich Blessing, photographer.

4: **Brown Rudnick Berlack Israels LLP,** New York, New York, Gensler, architect; ©Michael Moran Studio, photographer.

5: **Diageo,** North American Headquarters, Norwalk, Connecticut, CPG Architects, architect; ©Woodruff/Brown Architectural Photography, photographer.

6: **General Dynamics,** Headquarters, Fairview, Virginia, Lehman-Smith & McLeish, architect; ©Jon Miller/Hedrich Blessing, photographer.

5

SBLD Studio

Hospitality

Contrast, sparkle, color and focus are not common characteristics of most corporate lighting design projects, but these qualities are essential in defining the restaurants, hotels, multi-media conference centers and other hospitality facilities designed by SBLD Studio. Since the hospitality industry needs flexible environments that can be changed at the touch of a button, SBLD Studio employs such lighting tools as color-changing LED systems and sophisticated, programmable lighting controls that can transform the mood to match the moment. Whether the project area is part of a larger hospitality venue, such as a restaurant in a hotel, or a special amenity for a larger facility with a different overall mission, such as a dining room in a corporate headquarters, SBLD Studio is prepared to work with clients and their architects and interior designers to make everyone's guests feel welcome. That's how guests perceive the café/bar areas, conference center and dining area at the North American headquarters of Diageo, in Norwalk, Connecticut, and the Palette Restaurant & Bar at the Madison Hotel, in Washington, D.C., two recently completed hospitality projects by SBLD Studio that are illustrated here.

Sean O'Connor Associates

Los Angeles
8820 Wilshire Boulevard
Suite 320
Beverly Hills, CA 90211
310.659.5900
310.659.5915 (Fax)

Philadelphia
310 N. 11th Street
Fourth Floor
Philadelphia, PA 19107
215.988.9200
215.988.9008 (Fax)

www.seanoconnorassociates.com
info@seanoconnorassociates.com

Sean O'Connor Associates

Hospitality

Should tables be set for lunch or dinner? Will guest service stress luxury or value? In serving the hospitality business, Sean O'Connor Associates finds lighting design requires a thorough consideration of the multi-functional nature of clients' venues. By day, cafés, lounges and restaurants welcome you to evenly illuminated areas. By night, these same facilities employ pools of soft, warm light to create intimacy around you. At all times, the lighting must support the intent of the hospitality environment and respond to its architectural cues. For example, the transformation of Philadelphia's landmark Bellevue-Stratford into the Park Hyatt Philadelphia at the Bellevue (shown here) required lighting to support the interior design's unique old-and-new mix. The scheme brought sparkle and glamour to the Rose Garden Banquet Room with refinished and relamped chandeliers and decorative sconces plus remote-controlled, motorized accent lights. For XIX, the new oyster bar restaurant, set within a multi-tiered, domed room, a custom-designed "pearl necklace" chandelier highlights the soaring, 36-foot dome, custom MR16 halogen spotlights cantilevered over the edge of the cove beneath the dome make the raw bar below sparkle, and custom-designed, pearl-detailed sconces along the perimeter provide human scale and a romantic wash of light for the banquettes' guests.

1: **Fork Restaurant and Fork: Etc.,** Philadelphia, Pennsylvania, Marguerite Rodgers, Ltd., interior designer; Barry Halkin, photographer.

2: **Niebaum-Coppola,** Palo Alto, California, Arcanum Architecture, architect; Keith Cronin, photographer.

3, 4, 5: **Park Hyatt Philadelphia at the Bellevue,** Philadelphia, Pennsylvania, Studio Torres, architect; Marguerite Rodgers, Ltd., interior designer; Eric Laignel, photographer.

1

2

3

4

Sean O'Connor Associates

In the competitive retailing world, Sean O'Connor Associates conceives lighting designs that offer shoppers unique, brand-building shopping experiences. Such leading retailers (shown here) as Cingular, Functional Furnishings, Gap, Pottery Barn and Williams-Sonoma rely on the firm's solutions to enhance the definition and color of merchandise, conserve energy and reduce maintenance through the careful selection of lamps, luminaires and controls. For example, the three lighting prototypes it has developed for Cingular, one of numerous long-term clients, respond to changing marketing programs and architecture with distinctive designs—the version shown features custom-designed, rounded-end glowing slots and continuous valances—to provide a distinctive look while meeting stringent budgets. Lighting in Williams-Sonoma's prestigious New York store at Time Warner Center dramatizes a spectacular, two-story space with flexible, custom-designed display lighting that can be adjusted without a lift, custom-designed lighting slots incorporating air supply and return to eliminate grills and diffusers from the ceiling plane, and a dimming system. Custom-designed, back-lit fluorescent boxes in the vitrines and at the cashwrap use inexpensive materials to create elegant solutions for Functional Furnishings. And Gap's flagship store design employs a custom-designed metal panel ceiling system integrating recessed accent and down lighting with back-lit side panels to "float" not below the upper ceiling plane.

1: **Gap,** 5th and Pine, Seattle, Washington, Gap, Inc with Callison Architecture, architect; Gap, Inc., photographer.

2: **Williams-Sonoma,** Time Warner Center, New York, New York, Callison Architecture, architect; Aero Studios, Ltd., interior designer; Chris Eden/Callison, photographer.

3: **Cingular,** Atlanta, Georgia, Callison Architecture, architect; Chris Eden/Callison, photographer.

4: **Pottery Barn,** Palo Alto, California, Brand + Allen, architect; Mark Luthringer, photographer.

5: **Functional Furnishings,** Polaris, Columbus, Ohio, Jonathan Barnes: Architecture and Design, architect; Brad Feinknopf, photographer.

Sean O'Connor Associates

Residential

The lighting for a residence is as personal a choice for the homeowner as the architecture and interior design, so Sean O'Connor Associates works closely with homeowners and project teams to produce effective solutions. Modern homes tend to be brighter, whiter and more evenly illuminated with sheets of light, while traditional homes are generally warmer with pools of light. Yet both styles depend on incandescent and halogen lamps and a mix of decorative fixtures and architectural luminaires that blend with the environment and "disappear" whenever possible. As illustrated by two projects designed by Marguerite Rodgers, Ltd. as interior designer with Sean O'Connor Associates as

lighting designer, Chestnut Hill Residence, in Chestnut Hill, Pennsylvania, and the Shore House, in Loveladies, New Jersey (both shown here), good lighting is created space by space. While layers of halogen and incandescent lighting are used to dramatize the formal foyer of Chestnut Hill Residence, fiber optic lighting coupled to a halogen source, low-profile xenon strip lighting and sconces make the wine room glow without introducing heat or UV. By contrast, the understated and relaxed interior of the Shore House is characterized by custom-designed MR16 in-floor, up-lighting and a highly organized pattern of dimensional square MR16 Accent lights that marks a path through the house.

1

1, 3: Shore House, Loveladies, New Jersey, Marguerite Rodgers, Ltd., interior designer; Matt Wargo (living room), Barry Halkin (pool) photographers.

2, 4, 5: Chestnut Hill Residence, Chestnut Hill, Pennsylvania, Marguerite Rodgers, Ltd., interior designer; John Carnett (stair, guest house dining room), Barry Halkin (wine cellar), photographers.

Sean O'Connor Associates

Corporate/Institutional

1: Coventry, Corporate Offices, Fort Washington, Pennsylvania, Marguerite Rodgers, Ltd., interior designer; Matt Wargo, photographer.

2, 3: SmartWrap, Cooper-Hewitt National Design Museum, New York, New York, Kieran Timberlake Associates, architect; Barry Halkin, photographer.

When Sean O'Connor Associates designs lighting for corporate and institutional spaces, job tasks are not the only issues. With energy codes demanding lower lighting power densities, lamp efficacy and fixture selection receive closer scrutiny, linear fluorescent lamps are heavily used in conjunction with daylighting, and color temperatures are often selected based on available daylight. The need to illuminate space inside and outside the office is amply demonstrated by two contrasting projects (shown here) with lighting designed by Sean O'Connor Associates: Coventry, in Fort Washington, Pennsylvania, and SmartWrap, in New York. The lighting of Coventry's three-floor, 80,000-square-foot corporate headquarters relies on a select few sources, including tungsten, halogen, low-voltage xenon and fluorescent, to fulfill specific requirements. The lobbies, for example, use incandescent sources in recessed and custom shelf lighting details, providing a residential feel while energy efficient fluorescent fixtures serve the office spaces. The SmartWrap™ exhibit pavilion, erected in the garden of the Cooper Hewitt National Design Museum, showcases an experimental curtain wall material. SmartWrap™ consists of a polyethylene terephthalate (PET) skin that acts as a substrate for other layers incorporating climate control phase change materials, organic light-emitting diodes (OLEDs), organic photovoltaics, and organic thin-film transistor, which provides circuitry between these components. Its luminous floor and exhibit panels are lighted from within by dimmable strips of T8 lamps in a sunken pit. Its double helix exterior is illuminated by in-ground uplight fixtures with PAR20 and PAR30 halogen lamps.

Visual Terrain, Inc.

14141 Covello Street
Suite 4B
Van Nuys, CA 91405-1400
818.786.3500
818.786.3501 (Fax)
www.visualterrain.net
info@visualterrain.net

Visual Terrain, Inc.

Tourists in New York's Times Square, London's Piccadilly Circus or Tokyo's Ginza know that outdoor lighting can create a magical world at night. Since good outdoor lighting balances safety and security with mood, Visual Terrain seeks to simultaneously articulate the architecture and function of each outdoor project, create an inviting space for social interaction, establish a color palette inspired by architecture, landscaping and other surrounding elements, respect the rhythms of day and night as well as the seasons, and establish layers of light for aesthetics and function. Consider the firm's work at the 310-room Morongo Casino Resort & Spa, in Cabazon, California. The guest experience begins with the approach, a "big picture" vision of the building seemingly rising out of the desert, that plays light on the walls rather than the ground for visual impact. The façade lighting adopts a natural color spectrum of sunrise to sunset supplemented by additional LED accents tracing the flowing roofline. To avoid impeding the expansive guest view from the top-floor restaurant an

LED video display was integrated within the window mullions of the curtain wall at the tower's upper floors to provide memorable kinetic imagery for the finishing touch to the Morongo "brand."

1: Spotlight29, Coachella, California, SOSH Architects, architect; Andrea Piacentini Design Inc., interior designer; Tom Paiva, photographer.

2: Jimmy Buffett's Margaritaville Café, Myrtle Beach, South Carolina, The McBride Co., designer; Burroughs & Chapin, developer; Michael Gatewood/Mudpie Studios, photographer.

3: Mann Theatres, Aurora, Colorado, Penwal Industries, theming designer; Behr Bowers, architect; James Berchert, photographer.

4: LAX Gateway Enhancement, Los Angeles International Airport, Los Angeles, California, Ted Tokio Tanaka Architects, Nadel Architects, Inc., architects; Tom Paiva, photographer.

5: Morongo Casino Resort & Spa, Cabazon, California, The Jerde Partnership, Thalden-Boyd, architects; Tom Paiva, photographer.

Visual Terrain, Inc.

Eating out is increasingly about dining as an experience, and today's guest decides where to dine by considering the décor and service as well as the cuisine. Visual Terrain's approach to lighting dining spaces is thus based on supporting the dining experience sought by the restaurateur. Using lamps, fixtures and controls to implement the design, the firm develops a flexible response to the architecture and level of service that is both functional and atmospheric. Lighting for breakfast, for example, differs considerably from lighting for lunch or dinner, even though the consumption of food remains the major function at all hours. How effective lighting can be in evoking a mood can be seen at the new FireLake Grill House and Cocktail Bar, in Minneapolis. Recessed downlights, decorative pendant fixtures, cove lighting and other lighting solutions are combined to enhance the ambiance of the main dining room, bar, and two private dining rooms. These tools are used to illuminate

Dining Spaces

the plaster ceiling, highlight the activities of the chef in the exhibition kitchen, while meeting stringent health code requirements for food service and illuminating key architectural elements to convey the warm, gracious mood and Mediterranean design concept of the space—which the Twin Cities has kept full since opening day.

1: **FireLake Grill House and Cocktail Bar,** Minneapolis, Minnesota, Cuningham Group, architect; Sue Firestone and Associates, interior designer; Gallop Studios, photographer.

2, 4, 5: **Colusa Casino Resort,** Colusa, California, SOSH Architects, architect; Andrea Piacentini Design Inc., interior designer; Tom Paiva, photographer.

3, 6: **Crustacean,** Beverly Hills, California, Milan Architects, Inc., architect; Derek Rath, photographer.

1

2

3

4

5

6

Visual Terrain, Inc.

Ententaining Spaces

Storytelling becomes art in entertaining spaces, where architecture and lighting conjure make believe environments. Of course, the lighting designed by Visual Terrain for casinos, nightclubs, theaters, bowling alleys and the like must solve practical problems well, identifying stairs and exits while immersing the guest in the story of the space. The results can often be outstanding. The design by Visual Terrain for Silk the Club, a new, 28,000-square-foot nightclub at the 522-room Pechanga Resort & Casino, in Temecula, California, goes a step further than more conventional installations by creating almost an entire entertainment venue through light. Arriving guests encounter a long, curved main entry wall that changes color in response to their movements, followed by a small foyer of color-shifting columns divided by pure white, low-voltage uplights. This leads to the main space and mezzanine, showcasing such features as a stunning, 28-foot by 14-foot Fountain Chandelier of over 4,000 programmable, color-changing fiber optic strands above the main bar, floor-to-ceiling programmable LED fixtures and cylinders that wash the space with indirect lighting, an internally lit steel staircase, and low-voltage linear sources integrated into furniture and bar fascia. There are even granite bar tops with small, imbedded crystal LED uplights on which guests can rest their drinks.

Visual Terrain, Inc.

Working Spaces

Business managers may be surprised to learn that the lighting of working spaces is seldom purely a functional proposition. In fact, lighting projects undertaken by Visual Terrain for working spaces often deal with such issues as corporate culture, brand identity, employment policy and market positioning as well as job tasks. Lighting communicates to employees, vendors, shareholders and customers, demonstrating such intangibles as how companies feel about their products, what levels of goods and services customers will find, and where private transactions can be safely and securely conducted. In designing the lighting for the headquarters of Roland Corporation U.S., a leading manufacturer and distributor of Roland and BOSS electronic musical instruments, in Los Angeles, Visual Terrain created a lighting environment to reflect the high quality of the company's products. The elegant lighting of the facility not only showcases Roland's pianos, organs, keyboards, synthesizers, electronic percussion sets and more, it sets the tone for the company's well-established corporate culture, with indirect lighting reinforcing the facility's formal architecture and complementing the company's traditional way of doing business. Working in concert with the architecture, the lighting design clearly states that the outside world's hectic pace does not prevail in the world of Roland Corporation.

1, 2: Roland Corporation U.S., Los Angeles, California, Gensler, architect; Derek Rath, photographer.

3: Taryn Rose, Beverly Hills, California, Milan Architects, Inc., architect; Agave Studios, photographer.

4: Hollywood Vaults, Hollywood, California, Design Arc, architect; Tom Bonner, photographer.

Design
with Light.

New York Times Mock-up, College Point Queens, NY
Renzo Piano, Fox & Fowle – Architects
Gensler – Interiors

A New Vision

- AAC SolarTrac™ 3 WindowManagement™
  & Daylighting Automated Shade System
- Daylighting Controls
- Automated shade system & daylighting software
  maximize views and daylight while managing
  excessive glare and solar gain
- www.mechoshade.com

MechoShade®
The Architect's Choice.™

MechoShade Systems, Inc.
718-729-2020 • www.mechoshade.com

Quality vs. Quantity?

By Roger Yee

As lighting becomes increasingly critical to the man-made environment, a global energy crisis puts lighting designers in a difficult but promising position

Look at the young, excited faces in the crowds exploring the nightlife of such far-flung cities as London, Berlin, Abu Dhabi, Chennai, Shanghai, Los Angeles and New York, and you'll see why lighting designers like Jeffrey I.L. Miller, IALD feel so optimistic. "This is an amazing moment for lighting designers," says Miller, director of Pivotal Lighting Design at Affiliated Engineers NW, Inc. and president of the International Association of Lighting Designers (IALD). "Populations around the world are experiencing more professionally designed lighting than ever before. Our work is appreciated."

Architects, interior designers, landscape architects, city planners, and real estate developers, owners and managers are using lighting designers to do more than defy humankind's natural circadian rhythms as night falls, by keeping us busy working or playing when our ancestors would have been fast asleep. They are delivering quality light to places where natural light never intrudes, transforming the way we see the man-made environment, and making our days and nights more productive and enjoyable as a result. In the relatively brief interval since the incandescent bulb was perfected in 1879, and the fluorescent tube was introduced in 1939, the earth has increasingly become a continuously illuminated planet.

That much recent urban development has occurred with the participation of lighting designers whose identities remain entirely unknown to the public—while architects and interior designers enjoy an unprecedented level of visibility and even celebrity as "starchitects"—speaks volumes about the situation currently confronting these technically oriented and artistically inclined design professionals. Lighting designers are typically hired by other designers to serve and report to them rather than to the clients of construction projects. The lack of direct contact with clients or public recognition seems less distracting to them, however, than their place in the design process.

Above: Dublin Public Library, Dublin, California, BSA Architects, architect; Peters & Myer, lighting designer.

Why there's probably a lighting designer in your future

Kevin Flynn, AIA, IESNA, understands first-hand the predicament lighting designers face when they join building projects after major decisions have already been made about design, scheduling and budgets. An architect with extensive lighting design experience, Flynn is executive vice president of Kiku Obata & Company, an interior architecture firm, and president of the Illuminating Engineering Society of North America (IESNA), and readily admits that lighting does not enjoy high-priority status among architects. "There wasn't much on lighting at architecture school," Flynn recalls, "so I studied theater design to learn more."

It's hard to disagree when lighting designers insist lighting is a key element of architecture rather than an afterthought. "When you see great work, you know it's the result of an integrated process, like software," Miller indicates. "Lighting design is not a solo act. Ideally, it should be an integrative design process, iterative, integrated and overlapping."

Ironically, growing calls for zero-net energy design of buildings, bans on incandescent lighting, and even drastic cuts in energy usage for lighting may transform the lighting designer's strategic importance overnight. As the world struggles to secure energy supplies and reduce energy

consumption, the energy consumed by lighting has inevitably come under scrutiny. It's not small change. A 2002 Department of Energy study estimated that America's lighting consumes 8.2 quads (one quad equals 1015 BTUs), 765 TWh/yr (terawatt-hours per year) or about 22 percent of the nation's total electricity.

Where will the cuts be made, and how should they be executed? Lighting designers expect to be regularly invited to help craft successful, environmentally friendly solutions, adopting many concepts embodied in the U.S. Green Building Council's Leadership in Energy and Environmental Design (LEED) certification program. "For our business and me personally, embracing an environmental approach to design and construction makes a lot of sense," argues Mark Loeffler, IALD, LC, LEED. lighting design director of Atelier Ten, an engineering consulting firm, an instructor at New York's Parsons School of Design and an expert on environmental design. "The new spotlight on energy will guide us towards better lighting strategies and open up a dialogue between architects and lighting designers early in the design process."

Designing*with*LIGHT.com

Before you start your next lighting project.

Consider how much time you spend researching fixtures, estimating projects, collecting submittal data and keeping it organized. Designingwithlight.com is a revolutionary approach to managing your lighting projects. Quickly find the right products for your application; create, store and export fixture schedules; get budgetary pricing and lead-times – all in a personalized project workspace. Start your next project at DesigningwithLight.com today.

LIGHTOLIER®
Lighting that makes a difference.℠

The lamp that lights your way tomorrow

Even critics of former Vice President Al Gore and his Academy Award-winning documentary, An Inconvenient Truth, recognize that the ways in which the world produces and consumes lighting must inevitably change. Is the answer to turn off half the lights? Or invent a better light bulb?

Cutting waste seems like a sensible quick fix. But James Benya, FIALD, principal of Benya Lighting Design and an expert on energy conservation, cautions that energy savings from conservation won't come easily. "When people are unused to energy conservation it's hard to change their habits," he observes, citing America's infatuation with gas-guzzling SUVs.

"Now everyone likes the idea of net-zero energy consumption," Benya continues. "To approach this goal, we must conserve like hell and cut our plug loads." In the long term, he notes, LED technology promises greater energy efficiency, more compact equipment and cooler operations in perhaps five to 10 years. Meanwhile, there is plenty of good technology available. "We can make a difference right now," he declares. "Compact fluorescent lamps are convenient and reliable, and fluorescent tubes with ballasts could be better but they still beat incandescent, so let's use them. Motion sensors and other controls can also help if we put them where they make sense."

Benya and his colleagues are surprised at how little value has been placed on daylight until recently. "Daylight is quality light that's available to everyone," he notes, "and designing buildings to optimize it will let us turn off the lights. But you have to know how to design buildings for daylight. If your client ends up with excess glare and heat gain, daylight won't prove anything." Fortunately, lighting designers are trained to use daylight as well as electric light, which should earn them a coveted seat at the building team's table. "Daylighting plays to our strengths," Mark Loeffler points out.

Regardless of what the future holds, lighting designers appear to be entering an era that finally values them for their expertise and creativity. New technologies will someday give them new methods to portray the man-made world that architects and interior designers haven't even dreamed of. For now, their skills will be indispensable in saving our planet from ourselves. "Once new energy codes are passed, we'll get involved in projects at the start," states Kevin Flynn, "since architects and builders won't know what to do next."

Above: Benjamin Franklin Parkway, Façade and Sculpture Lighting, Philadelphia, Pennsylvania, Cope Linder Architects, architect; The Lighting Practice, lighting designer.

Resources*

195 CHOP
Lighting Design: The Lighting Practice
Translight, Advance Digital & Screen Printing

350 Madison Avenue, New York, NY
Lighting Design: SBLD Studio
Linear Lighting

2100 Ponce de Leon, Coral Gables, FL
Lighting Design: Brilliant Lighting Design
Wide Lite, Ruud

Acadia University, K.C. Irving Environmental Science Center
Lighting Design: Ann Kale Associates, Ltd.
Unilight, Lutron, Louis Poulsen, Portfolio, Metalux, Litecontrol

American Airlines Admirals Club, Dallas/Fort Worth International Airport, DFW Airport, TX
Lighting Design: Bouyea & Associates
Kurt Versen, Neotek, Belfer Lighting

American Savings Bank, Executive Offices, Honolulu, HI
Lighting Design: h.e. banks + associates Lighting Design
Cooper Portfolio, Corelite, Legion, Leucos

American Savings Bank, Flagship Branch, Honolulu, HI
Lighting Design: h.e. banks + associates Lighting Design
Shaper Lighting, Corelite, Legion, Kurt Versen, Focal Point, Belfer, Flos

Argosy Casino, Riverside, MO
Lighting Design: Gallegos Lighting Design
Lighting Services Inc., Electronic Theatre Controls, International Ironworks, Arte de Mexico, Indy Lighting, Visual Lighting Technologies, High End Systems, BK Lighting, Rosco, ERCO, Juno, Hevi Lite, Translite Sonoma, Altman, Hydrel, Lumiere, Winona, Kim, Edison Price, BK Lighting, Quality, Indy, Phoenix, Northstar, Coemar, Birket Engineering, Designplan, Color Kinetics, Tokistar, Sun Valley Lighting, Casa Talamantes, Neri, Global, GE, Philips

Ayava Communications, Basking Ridge, NJ
Lighting Design: SBLD Studio
Zumtobel Staff Lighting, Lightolier, Se'lux, USA Illuminations, Lite Control, Ledalite, RSA Lighting, Luton (Controls)

Baltimore Visitors Center, Baltimore, MD
Lighting Design: C.M. Kling & Associates, Inc.
Hydrel, Hess America, Litelab

Banco Popular Center, San Juan, PR
Lighting Design: Brilliant Lighting Design
Lithonia

Bascillica Don Bosco, Panama City, Panama
Lighting Design: Brilliant Lighting Design
GE Lighting Systemss

Benaroya Symphony Hall, Seattle, WA
Lighting Design: Horton Lees Brogden Lighting Design
Taylor Stokes, Staff Lighting, Belfer Lighting, ETC, Lumiere, Kurt
Versen, Hydrel, General Electric Company, Philips Lighting Company, Lutron

Ben Gurion International Airport, Airside Terminal, Tel Aviv, Israel
Lighting Design: Horton Lees Brogden Lighting Design
Trilux, We-Ef

BF Parkway
Lighting Design: The Lighting Practice
ARC Lighting Systems, We'ef, BK Lighting, Windirect

The Borgata Hotel, Casino & Spa, Atlantic City, NJ
Lighting Design: Lighting Design Alliance
Lightolier, Lutron, Tokistar, Targetti, Eureka, Color Kinetics

Bridge of the Americas, Canal Zone, Rep. of Panama
Lighting Design: Brilliant Lighting Design
General Electric

Brooks/World Com hdqtrs, St. Louis, MO
Lighting Design: SBLD Studio
Kim Lighting, Bega, Neo-Ray Lighting

Brown Rudnick Berlack Israels LLP, New York, NY
Lighting Design: SBLD Studio
Mark Lighting, Kurt Versen, Louis Poulsen Lighting

Brown Thomas & Co., Dublin, Ireland
Lighting Design: Lightbrigade
Ushio, iGuzzini, RSA, Thorn Lighting

Burek Residence, Coconut Grove, FL
Lighting Design: Brilliant Lighting Design
Lumiere

California Aerospace Museum, Los Angeles, CA
Lighting Design: Gallegos Lighting Design
Rosco, Strand, GE, Philips

Caltrans District 7 Headquarters,
Los Angeles, CA
Lighting Design: Horton Lees Brogden Lighting Design
Paramount, Ledalite Architectural Products, Daybrite, KV, Prudential
Lighting, Lutron, Focal Point, Bega, NSI, Lumiere, Osram Sylvania

Camp Menehune
Lighting Design: Lang Lighting Design Inc.
ERCO Lighting, Lutron, Lucifer, GE

Centro Sambil Galleria Cascades, Caracas, Venezuela
Lighting Design: Brilliant Lighting Design
Ruud, Bronzelite

Changi Airport, Airport Rail Station, Singapore
Lighting Design: SBLD Studio
ERCO, Zumtobel Staff Lighting

Charlotte Douglas International Airport,
West Daily Parking Deck, Charlotte, NC
Lighting Design: C.M. Kling & Associates, Inc.
Wide-Lite, Solera, Daybrite, Forum, Gardco

The Cheesecake Factory, Nationwide
Lighting Design: Lighting Design Alliance
Lightolier, NSI, Innovative, Tokistar, Hydrel, Hevi-Lite, BK Lighting, Spectrum Lighting, Sternberg

Chestnut Hill Residence
Lighting Design: Sean O'Connor Associates
RSA Lighting, Lucifer Lighting, Specialty Lighting Industries, Nulux, Baldinger, BK Lighting, Erco, Q-Tran, Lutron

Christopher B. Smith Rafael Film Center
Lighting Design: O'Mahony & Myer
Taylor/Stokes Lighting, Prescolite, LSI Lighting

Cingular
Lighting Design: Sean O'Connor Associates
Bartco Lighting, Prescolite, Lightolier, RSA Lighting, Resolute

*An Incomplete list of major sources.
For more information please call design firms.

208

Cisco Systems, Customer Briefing Center,
New York, NY
Lighting Design: h.e. banks + associates
Lighting Design Osram Sylvania, Birchwood
Lighting

Cisco Systems, Executive Briefing Center,
San Jose, CA
Lighting Design: h.e. banks + associates
Lighting Design
Color Kinetics, Illuminating Experiences, Osram
Sylvania, Louis Poulsen, Gammalux, RSA
Lighting, H.E. Williams, Wila

Clay Center
Lighting Design: The Lighting Practice
Fiber Star, Winona, Edison Price, Ellipitipar

Club Prive
Lighting Design: Ann Kale Associates, Ltd.
Lucifer Lighting, Celestial Lighting

Colorado Ocean Journey, Denver, CO
Lighting Design: Gallegos Lighting Design
Northstar, Quality, Electronic Theatre Controls,
Times Square, Hydrel, Great American Market,
Diversitronics, Fiberstars, Tokistar, Lutron, GE,
Philips

Colpatria Tower, Bogota, Colombia
Lighting Design: Brilliant Lighting Design
Space Cannon

Colusa Casino Resort
Lighting Design: Visual Terrain, Inc.
Juno, Elliptipar, Finelite, Hevi Lite, Lumascape,
Times Square Lighting

Computer Science Corporation
Lighting Design: Ann Kale Associates, Ltd.
Lightolier, Lighting Services Inc., Kurt Versen

Contemporary Residence, Toronto, ON
Lighting Design: Lightbrigade
Osram Sylvania, Ingo Mauer, Martini, Blauet,
Ardee, Flos, Eureka

Coventry
Lighting Design: Sean O'Connor Associates
Kurt Versen, Lucifer Lighting, Belfer, Gammalux,
Bartco Lighting, Lithonia, Specialty Lighting
Industries, Q-Tran, Lutron

Crown Casino Continental Riande Hotel,
Panama City, Rep. of Panama
Lighting Design: Brilliant Lighting Design
Space Cannon, Cooper

Crustacean
Lighting Design: Visual Terrain, Inc.
Juno, Lumiere

**Denver Performing Arts Center, Ellie
Caulkins Opera House,** Denver, CO
Lighting Design: Horton Lees Brogden Lighting
Design
Winona Lighting, Ardee Lighting, Lumascape,
SistemaLux, B-K Lighting, ETC, Fiberstars,
Translite Sonoma, Eureka Lighting, USA
Illumination

Diageo, North American Headquarters,
Norwalk, CT
Lighting Design: SBLD Studio
Color Kinetics, USA Illumination, Electrix, Tech
Lighting, Neidhardt, Flos, Ochre

Dublin Library
Lighting Design: O'Mahony & Myer
Dual-Lite, Prescolite, Zumtobel, Peerless, Louis
Poulsen, Focal Point, Wellmade, Alkco, Columbia,
Visa, Corelite, Ellipitipar, Belfer, Color Kinetics,
Gardco, Sistemalux, Lightolier, Architectural Area
Lighting, KIM Lighting, McPhilben, BK Lighting,
Bega

Eiber Residence, Miami Beach, FL
Lighting Design: Brilliant Lighting Design
Ruud, Kim

Endeavor Talent Agency, Beverly Hills, CA
Lighting Design: Lighting Design Alliance
Delray Lighting, Lightolier, Alera Lighting, Bartco
Lighting, Wila Lighting, Luceplan, Artemide,
Ellipitipar

Essex County Courthouse
Lighting Design: Ann Kale Associates, Ltd.
McNicholas Lighting Restoration, Lucifer
Lighting, Lighting Services Inc., Specialty Lighting
Industries, Sylvania, Metalux

Fairmont Scottsdale Princess, Willow Stream
Spa, Scottsdale, AZ
Lighting Design: Bouyea & Associates
Kurt Versen, Neotek, Belfer Lighting

FireLake Grill House and Cocktail Bar
Lighting Design: Visual Terrain, Inc.
Cooper Lighting, Tokistar Lighting

Florida Aquarium, Tampa, FL
Lighting Design: Gallegos Lighting Design
Altman, Northstar, Quality, Times Square,
Columbia, GE, Philips

Fork Resturant
Lighting Design: Sean O'Connor Associates
Lucifer Lighting, Celestial Lighting, ELP , BK
Lighting, Lutron

Four Seasons Doha
Lighting Design: Lang Lighting Design Inc.
Lutron, Osram, ERCO, Ardee Lightinnnng

Four Seasons Resort Hualalai, Ka'upulehu, HI
Lighting Design: Bouyea & Associates
BK Lighting, Hydrel Lighting, Lightolier

Four Seasons Resort Whistler, Blackcomb,
BC, Canada
Lighting Design: Bouyea & Associates
BK Lighting, Belfer Lighting, Neotek, Kurt Versen

Four Seasons Troon
Lighting Design: Lang Lighting Design Inc.
Kurt Versen, Lutron, Cooper Lighting, Lumiere,
Neotek, BK Lighting, Hydrel, GE

Frist Center for the Visual Arts, Nashville, TN
Lighting Design: SBLD Studio
Rambusch Lighting, USA Illumination, Bega

Functional Furnishings
Lighting Design: Sean O'Connor Associates
Bartco Lighting, Alera, LiteLab, Prescolite,
Celestial Lighting

GameWorks at the Pike
Lighting Design: Visual Terrain, Inc.
High End Systems, Wildfire

Game Works - Easton
Lighting Design: Visual Terrain, Inc.
Color Kinetics, ETC, High End Systems, Juno, TPR
Enterprises LTD

The Gap
Lighting Design: Sean O'Connor Associates
Kurt Versen, Con-Tech, LiteLab, Peerless,
Specialty Lighting Industries, Ellipitipar, Lutron

General Dynamics, Hdqtrs, Fairview, VA (Alina)
Lighting Design: SBLD Studio
Mark Lighting, USA Illumination, Legion, RSA

George Washington Bridge
Lighting Design: Domingo Gonzalez Associates
GE Lighting Systems, Bega

Georgia State Capitol, Atlanta, GA
Lighting Design: Brilliant Lighting Design
GE, Ruud

Golden Moon Hotel & Casino, Philadelphia, MS
Lighting Design: Brilliant Lighting Design
Ruud, Sentinal Lighting, Cresent, Starfield

Golden State Museum, Sacramento, CA
Lighting Design: Gallegos Lighting Design
Electronic Theatre Controls, Strand, Rosco,
Prescolite, CSL, Light Project, Translite, Elliptipar,
Trend, Bega, Casa Talamantes, Ardee, GE, Philips

Grand River Regional Cancer Centre,
Kitchener, ON
Lighting Design: Lightbrigade
Osram/Sylvania, SPI, Arealite, Litecontrol, Mark
Lighting, Metalumen

Gulf State Park Beach Pavilion, Gulf Shores, AL
Lighting Design: C.M. Kling & Associates, Inc.
Louis Poulsen, Elliptipar

Hertz Orlando
Lighting Design: Domingo Gonzalez Associates
Kim Lighting

Hilton Boston Logan Airport, Boston, MA
Lighting Design: C.M. Kling & Associates, Inc.
ETC

**Hollywood Entertainment Museum and
Education Center for the Entertainment
Arts,** Hollywood, CA
Lighting Design: Gallegos Lighting Design
Electronic Theatre Controls, Rosco, Irideon,
Lighting Services Inc., Halo, Lithonia, Columbia,
Martin, Altman, GE, Philips

Hollywood Vaults
Lighting Design: Visual Terrain, Inc.
Lightolier

Holt Renfrew, Bloor Street, Toronto, ON
Lighting Design: Lightbrigade
Osram/Sylvania, Cooper Lighting, Lighting
Nelson & Garrett, Fiberstars, RSA, Litelab

Houston Galleria
Lighting Design: The Lighting Practice
RSA Lighting, Winona, LiteMakers, LiteLab, Noral,
National Cathode, Sterner, Indy, Engineered
Lighting Products, Windirect, Altman Lighting,
Rosco, Spectrum

Hudson River Park
Lighting Design: Domingo Gonzalez
Associates
Light Forms, Kim Lighting, Killark, Se'lux, Spring
City, C.W. Cole

Institute of International Economics,
Washington, DC
Lighting Design: C.M. Kling & Associates, Inc.
Erco, Kurt Versen, Zumtobel, NuArt,
KramInterContinental Hotel Toronto
Centre,Toronto, ON
Lighting Design: Lightbrigade
Osram/Sylvania, Insight Lighting, Zumtobel,
Eureka, Cooper, Lighting Nelson & Garrett

Jester Lounge, Panama City, Rep. of Panama
Lighting Design: Brilliant Lighting Design
Metalux

JFK International Airport, Arrivals Terminal 4,
Jamaica, NY
Lighting Design: SBLD Studio
Forum Lighting, Edison Price, Lighting Services Inc.

JFK Light Rail System
Lighting Design: Domingo Gonzalez Associates
Zumtobel, Icon International, Kim Lighting

JFK Terminal One
Lighting Design: Domingo Gonzalez Associates
Lightolier, Quality, Kurt Versen, Mark
Architectural Lighting, Zumtobel, Artemis
Lighting, Kim Lighting

Jimmy Buffett's Margaritaville Café
Lighting Design: Visual Terrain, Inc.
Spero Lighting, Tokistar

Johnson & Johnson
Lighting Design: The Lighting Practice
Halo, Neoray, Zumtobel

Kirkpatrick & Lockhart, New York, NY
Lighting Design: SBLD Studio
Linear Lighting, Legion, USA Illumination

Knoxville Convention Center, Knoxville, TN
Lighting Design: C.M. Kling & Associates, Inc.
Kurt Versen, Fiberstars, Bega, Litelab

La Maison Simons, Laval, QC
Lighting Design: Lightbrigade
GE, Indy Lighting, Boca Flasher, Lithonia
Lighting, Zumtobel/Staff, RSA, Bruck Lighting

Lane Avenue Bridge, Columbus, OH
Lighting Design: Brilliant Lighting Design
Hydrel

Lehman-Smith + McLeish, Washington, DC
Lighting Design: SBLD Studio
Nippo, USA Illumination, Mark Lighting, Specialty
Lighting Industries, Erco, Se'lux

Long Beach Aquarium, Long Beach, CA
Lighting Design: Gallegos Lighting Design
Electronic Theatre Controls, Rosco, GAM, Strand,
Sterner, Kim, Louis Poulsen, Altman, Orgatec
Omegalux, Elliptipar, Northstar, Times Square,
Lighting Services Inc., Abolite, Lumiere, Lithonia,
Lumenyte, GE, Philips

**Los Angeles City Hall, Exterior Historic
Renovation,** Los Angeles, CA
Lighting Design: Horton Lees Brogden Lighting
Design
Hydrel, Phoenix Lighting, Venture Lamps, B-K
Lighting

Los Angeles International Airport Gateway
Lighting Design: Visual Terrain, Inc.
Altman, Martin, Wybron Inc.

**Los Angeles Metro Rail Vermont/Santa
Monica Station,** Los Angeles, CA
Lighting Design: Horton Lees Brogden Lighting
Design
Bega, CW Cole

Lyons Hair Salon, South Miami, FL
Lighting Design: Brilliant Lighting Design
Metallux

MacArthur Causeway Bridge, Miami, FL
Lighting Design: Brilliant Lighting Design
Wide Lite

Magnet, San Francisco, CA
Lighting Design: h.e. banks + associates
Lighting Design
Columbia, Tech Lighting, Peerlit

Mann Theatres
Lighting Design: Visual Terrain, Inc.
Lighting Services, Inc., Lumiere, Sun Valley
Lighting

Marriott World Center Orlando, Orlando, FL
Lighting Design: C.M. Kling & Associates, Inc.
RSA Lighting, Rambusch, Kurt Versen, Strand

McKinsey
Lighting Design: The Lighting Practice
Kurt Versen, Zumtobel, Focal Point, Eureka

Meaders Residence
Lighting Design: Lang Lighting Design Inc.
Lightolier, Lutron, GE, Cooper, Energie, Lucifer,
Belfer, Translite-Sonoma

Medimmune, Gaithersburg, MD
Lighting Design: C.M. Kling & Associates, Inc.
Zumtobel, Bruck, Kurt Versen, Edison Price, Steng

MetLife Tower, New York, NY
Lighting Design: Horton Lees Brogden Lighting Design
Sterner Lighting/MDI, Visual Lighting Technologies, Special-T
Lighting, A+L Lighting Corporation, Horizon Control, Inc.

Midori Galleries, Coconut Grove, FL
Lighting Design: Brilliant Lighting Design
Cooper Lighting

Moët Hennessy, New York, NY
Lighting Design: Horton Lees Brogden Lighting Design
Linear Lighting, Lightolier, Tech Lighting, Lucifer Lighting, Delray Lighting, Flos, Plug Lighting, Big Bang, Martin Architectural, Luceplan, Prudential Lighting, Alkco Lighting, Illuminating Experiences, Elliptipar, Litecontrol,

Monterey Bay Aquarium, Monterey, CA
Lighting Design: Gallegos Lighting Design
Lighting Services Inc, Luminis, Winona, Lithonia, Elliptipar, Peerless, GE, Philips

Morongo Casino Resort & Spa
Lighting Design: Visual Terrain, Inc.
Element Labs, Elliptipar, iLight, Martin, Northstar/Thorn

Morongo Casino Resort & Spa - Interiors
Lighting Design: Visual Terrain, Inc.
Architectural Cathode, Birchwood, Color Kinetics, Leviton, Metalux, Portfolio, RSA, Spectrum, Tokistar, Visa

Mount Tiburon Residence, Tiburon, CA
Lighting Design: h.e. banks + associates Lighting Design
Akari, CX Lighting, Phoenix Day, Lightolier, Ardee Clickstrip

MTV On Line, New York, NY
Lighting Design: Horton Lees Brogden Lighting Design
Lightolier, Belfer Lighting, Legion Lighting, Leviton, Exceline, Tech
Lighting, General Electric, Luminary Tools, Special FX Lighting

Nasher Sculpture Center, Garden, Dallas, TX
Lighting Design: Horton Lees Brogden Lighting Design
B-K Lighting, Hydrel, Elliptipar, Kim Lighting, Bega, Semper Fi Power Supply Inc, PEM Equipment Company

National Sanctuary Church, Panama City, Panama
Lighting Design: Brilliant Lighting Design
Stonco, GE

The National World War II Memorial, Washington, DC
Lighting Design: Horton Lees Brogden Lighting Design
Exterior Verte, Hydrel, Sterner

Niebaum-Coppola
Lighting Design: Sean O'Connor Associates
RSA Lighting, Lightolier, Celestial Lighting, Lutron

Netflix
Lighting Design: Luminae Souter Associates, LLC
Delray, Lightolier, ERCO, Systemlux, Prudential, LumenArt, , Louis Poulsen, Lightolier, Leucos, Bruck, Focalpoint

New York Botanical Gardens Visitors' Center
Lighting Design: Domingo Gonzalez Associates
A&L Lighting, Lumiere, Forms + Surfaces, Linear Lighting, Bruck

New York Historical Society
Lighting Design: Domingo Gonzalez Associates
LSI Lighting Solutions, Rejuvenation, Neo-Ray, Specialty Lighting, Winona Lighting, Edison Price Lighting, A&L Lighting

New York State Appellate Court
Lighting Design: Domingo Gonzalez Associates
Edison Price Lighting, A&L Lighting, EDI, Winona

Novartis Institute for Functional Genomics, La Jolla, CA
Lighting Design: Horton Lees Brogden Lighting Design
B-K Lighting, LiteControl, Hydrel, Cole Lighting, Insight, HE Williams, Hess America

Olio
Lighting Design: Ann Kale Associates, Ltd.
T.A. Greene Co., Lucifer Lighting, Halo, Color Kinetics, Light Solutions

One Ten Lincoln Street, Boston, MA
Lighting Design: C.M. Kling & Associates, Inc.
Baldinger, Lightolier

The Palette Restaurant & Bar, The Madison Hotel, Washington, DC
Lighting Design: SBLD Studio
Tech Lighting, Belfer, RSA Lighting

Park Hyatt Philadelphia at the Bellevue
Lighting Design: Sean O'Connor Associates
Specialty Lighting Industries, Lucifer Lighting, Lumid, Ardee, Celestial Lighting, LiteLab, RC Lighting, Q-Tran, Lutron

Penthouse Residence at the Four Seasons Hotel, San Francisco, CA
Lighting Design: h.e. banks + associates Lighting Design
CJ Lighting, Ardee Clickstrip, Litelab, Venini, Optic Arts

Per se
Lighting Design: Ann Kale Associates, Ltd.
Lucifer Lighting, Baldinger, Litelab, Lightolier, Flexilight, BSCM

Pier One, Adaptive Reuse, San Francisco, CA
Lighting Design: Horton Lees Brogden Lighting Design
Elliptipar, Lite Control, Lightolier, Zumbotel Staff, Modular, Light Lab, DayBrite, Louis Poulson, Shaper, Hydrel, Bega, B-K Lighting, Lumiere, Linear Lighting, Translite, Eureka, Corelite, Lutron

Port of Los Angeles, San Pedro, CA
Lighting Design: Lighting Design Alliance
Holophane, Cole Lighting, AAL, Selux, Hydrel, Sterner, Tokistar

Pottery Barn
Lighting Design: Sean O'Connor Associates
Kurt Versen, RSA Lighting, Celestial Lighting, Lucifer Lighting, Ardee, Lutron

Prime Outlets San Marcos
Lighting Design: The Lighting Practice
Lumec, Neri, Gardco, Bega, Insight, Color Kinetics, BK Lighting

Private residence, Canada
Lighting Design: Lightbrigade
Osram/Sylvania, Martini, Eureka, Dale Chihuly Studio, Artemide, Bruck Lighting

Private residence, modern
Lighting Design: Bouyea & Associates
Edison Price Lighting, Thomas Grant, Don Embree, Orion Antiques

Private residence, San Francisco, CA
Lighting Design: Luminae Souter Associates, LLC
RSA Lighting, LBL Lighting, Eureka, IRIS, Artemide

Private residence, traditional
Lighting Design: Bouyea & Associates
Lighting Services Inc, Kurt Versen, Belfer Lighting

RayKo Photo Center, San Francisco, CA
Lighting Design: h.e. banks + associates Lighting Design
Birchwood Lighting, Halo

Reynolda House Museum of American Art,
Mary & Charles Babcock Wing, Winston-Salem, NC
Lighting Design: SBLD Studio
Lighting Services Inc., Louis Poulsen Lighting, USA Illumination, Flos Lighting, Finelite, Zumtobel Staff, Lithonia, ETC Inc. (Controls)

Ritz-Carlton Central Park South, New York, NY
Lighting Design: Bouyea & Associates
Kurt Versen, Ardee Lighting

Roland US Headquarters
Lighting Design: Visual Terrain, Inc.
Architectural Cathode, Cooper Lighting, ETC, Flos, Lightolier

Ronald Reagan Washington National Airport, Washington, DC
Lighting Design: Horton Lees Brogden Lighting Design
Lightolier, Edison Price Inc, Forum Lighting, Kurt Versen Inc., Litecontrol

Ruth's Chris Roseville
Lighting Design: Fox and Fox Design
Eric Industries, Tech Lighting, Glass Illuminations, Kurt Versen, Tokistar, B-K Lighting, RSA Lighting, Lutron

Ruth's Chris Sacramento,
Lighting Design: Fox and Fox Design
Lutron, Rock Cottage, Martini, Kurt Versen, Tech Lighting, RSA Lighting

Sammy's Studio
Lighting Design: Fox and Fox Design
Eric Industries, Lightolier, NSI, Tokistar, Spectrum, Lucifer

San Francisco City Hall, San Francisco, CA
Lighting Design: Horton Lees Brogden Lighting Design
Taylor Stokes, Scott Architectural Lighting, Lite Lab, Kurt Versen, Peerless, Rejuvenation, H.E. Williams, Zumtobel Staff, Linear Lighting, Alkco, Phoenix, Hydrel, Strand

Santana Row, San Jose, CA
Lighting Design: Horton Lees Brogden Lighting Design
King Luminaire, Architectural Area Lighting, Winona, Bega, Cooper, Lightolier, Bartco Lighting, Delray, Shaper, Evergreen, Scott Architectural, T.A. Green Company, We-ef,

Sistemalux, Primus, B-K Lighting, Hydrel, Teka, Pauluhn, IE, DeMajo Polipo, Fail Safe, Luxo, Artimede, Creative Lighting Systems, Compass, Bevolo, Visa, Contrast Lighting, Light Way, Nova Lighting

Schermerhorn Symphony Hall, Nashville, TN
Lighting Design: SBLD Studio
Crenshaw Lighting, USA Illumination, Louis Poulsen Lighting

Seattle Opera House, Marion Oliver McCaw Hall, Seattle, WA
Lighting Design: Horton Lees Brogden Lighting Design
Lucifer Lighting, Ortek, Primus, Rambusch Lighting, Lighting Services, Inc., Edison Price Lighting, Belfer Lighting, Lumiere

Secaucus Junction
Lighting Design: Domingo Gonzalez Associates
Kurtzon Lighting, Icon International, KIM Lighting, Metalumen, Kurt Versen, Spring City, Edison Price Lighting

Shelby St. Bridge
Lighting Design: Domingo Gonzalez Associates
Wide Lite, GE Lighting Systems, Luminis, Spaulding

Shepard Hall at City College of New York
Lighting Design: Domingo Gonzalez Associates
Winona, EDI, Litemakers, Canlet

Sheraton Biscayne Bay, Miami, FL
Lighting Design: Brilliant Lighting Design
GE, Hydrel

Shore House
Lighting Design: Sean O'Connor Associates
Specialty Lighting Industries, Lucifer Lighting, RSA Lighting, Light Project, DesignPlan, Louis Poulsen, Bega, Hess, Q-Tran, Lutron

Silk the Club - Pechanga Casino
Lighting Design: Visual Terrain, Inc.
Color Kinetics, Hevi Lite, Island Systems Design, Martin, Technifex, TIR Systems, Tokistar

SmartWrap
Lighting Design: Sean O'Connor Associates
Celestial, Erco, Lutron, GE

Southwest Museum, Los Angeles, CA
Lighting Design: Gallegos Lighting Design
Electronic Theatre Controls, Rosco, Lighting Services Inc., Iris, Philips

Spotlight29
Lighting Design: Visual Terrain, Inc.
Hevi Lite, Hydrel

Starwood Sheraton Centre Toronto
Lighting Design: Lighting Design Solutions/ H.H. Angus and Associates Limited
Architectural Area Lighting, Barbican Architectural Products, Lightolier, Strand Lighting, 3G Lighting

Sterner Automation, industrial office, Toronto, ON
Lighting Design: Lightbrigade
Philips, Osram/Sylvania, Axis Lighting, Artemide, Biffi, Eurolite

St. John the Divine Exhibit
Lighting Design: Domingo Gonzalez Associates
Tech Lighting

St. Francis Winery
Lighting Design: O'Mahony & Myer
Hans Duus Blacksmith, Inc., BK Lighting, Alkco, Prescolite, Hydrel, Hadco, KIM Lighting, Bega, Shaper Lighting, Elliptipar, Wellmade, Orgatech/ Omegalux, Columbia, Lightolier, Sterner, Saunders-Roe

Suba
Lighting Design: Ann Kale Associates, Ltd.
Hydrel, Halo

Taryn Rose
Lighting Design: Visual Terrain, Inc.
Bartco Lighting

TD Securities
Lighting Design: Lighting Design Solutions/ H.H. Angus and Associates Limited
Lightolier, Lutron, Nessen & Reggiani

TIAA Lobby
Lighting Design: Domingo Gonzalez Associates
Litelab, Icon International, A&L Lighting

Toronto Dominion Bank Executive Offices, Toronto, ON
Lighting Design: Lightbrigade
Philips, Litecontrol, Indy Lighting, Lightolier, Eurolite

Toronto General Hospital
Lighting Design: Lighting Design Solutions/ H.H. Angus and Associates Limited
Cooper, Fail-Safe, Heraeus, Zumtobel

Torre Global, Panama City, Rep. of Panama
Lighting Design: Brilliant Lighting Design
GE, Lumark

Towers Perrin, Stamford, CT
Lighting Design: SBLD Studio
Belfer Lighting, USA Illumination

Traditional residence, dining room, Toronto, ON
Lighting Design: Lightbrigade
GE Lighting, Lightolier, Sirmos

UBS Houston, Houston, TX
Lighting Design: Lang Lighting Design Inc.
Focal Point, Belfer, Lutron, Ledalite, Prescolite,
Ardee Lighting, Osram/Sylvania

University of Toronto
Lighting Design: Lighting Design Solutions/
H.H. Angus and Associates Limited
Baga/Feralux, Lightolier, Limburg, Metalumen,
RAB/Design, Se'Lux/Sill

**Utah State University, Manon Caine
Russell Kathryn Caine Wanlass
Performance Hall,** Logan, UT
Lighting Design: Horton Lees Brogden Lighting
Design
Lightolier, B-K Lighting, RSA, Litelab, Lucifer
Lighting with Q-tran transformers, Flos, Leucos,
Delray Lighting

Villa Regina Condominium, Miami, FL
Lighting Design: Brilliant Lighting Design
GE

VUE Condominium, Miami, FL
Lighting Design: Brilliant Lighting Design
GE, Ruud, Spectrum Lighting

Waldorf-Astoria, New York, NY
Lighting Design: C.M. Kling & Associates, Inc.
Lightolier, Kurt Versen, Strand

Waldorf-Astoria, Peacock Alley, New York, NY
Lighting Design: C.M. Kling & Associates, Inc.
Lightolier, RSA lighting, Lutron

Warner Bros. Movie World Madrid, Madrid,
Spain
Lighting Design: Gallegos Lighting Dessssign
Robers, Lutron, Electronic Theatre Controls, Erco,
GE, Philips

Washington, DC Convention Center,
Washington, DC
Lighting Design: C.M. Kling & Associates, Inc.
Lightolier, Hydrel, ETC, Lutron

Washington Square Arch
Lighting Design: Domingo Gonzalez Associates
GE Lighting Systems, KIM Lighting, Icon
International

West Side Ferry Terminal
Lighting Design: Domingo Gonzalez Associates
WE-EE, Zumtobel, Winona, C.W. Cole, Metalux,
Litelab, Se'lux, GE Lighting Systems, A&L Lighting

Westin Palo Alto
Lighting Design: Luminae Souter Associates, LLC
Niedhardt, Prescolite, Bronzlite, Nova Industries,
ELA Lighting, Prescolite, Alexandra

**Williams College, Williams College '62
Center for Theatre & Dance,** Williamstown, MA
Lighting Design: Horton Lees Brogden Lighting
Design
Lightolier, Translite, Sonoma, Microspot, Starfire
Lighting, Kirlin, Stonco, Linear Lighting, Delray
Lighting, RSA Lighting, Insight Lighting,
Spero Indy Lighting

Williams-Sonoma
Lighting Design: Sean O'Connor Associates
LiteLab, Kurt Versen, Celestial Lightin, Lightolier,
Bartco Lighting, Ardee, Q-Tran, Lutron

**Windsor Regional Cancer Centre, radiation
therapy treatment room,** Windsor, ON
Lighting Design: Lightbrigade
GE Lighting, Lightolier, Eurolite, Eureka, Hemera

Wooly Mammoth Theater, auditorium,
Washington, DC
Lighting Design: C.M. Kling & Associates, Inc.
Tech Lighting, Stonco, ETC

WTC Temporary PATH Station
Lighting Design: Domingo Gonzalez Associates
Holophane, Neo-Ray, Mercury Lighting
Products, Day-Brite, GE Lighting Systems, Icon
International, KIM Lighting

KEEP UP

JUNE 11-13, 2007 • CHICAGO
THE MERCHANDISE MART

FEATURING:
BUILDINGS SHOW®   OFFICE EXPO BY OFDA   TECHNOCON™
NEWHOSPITALITY   GREEN*LIFE*™
FINE DESIGN RESIDENTIAL FURNISHINGS SHOW™
ARCHITECTURAL STONE AND CERAMIC TILE EXPOSITION (ASCTEX)

NEOCON.COM

The Merchandise Mart

Index by Project

The Designer Series

Visual Reference Publications, Inc.

302 Fifth Avenue, New York, NY 10001
212.279.7000 • Fax 212.279.7014
www.visualreference.com

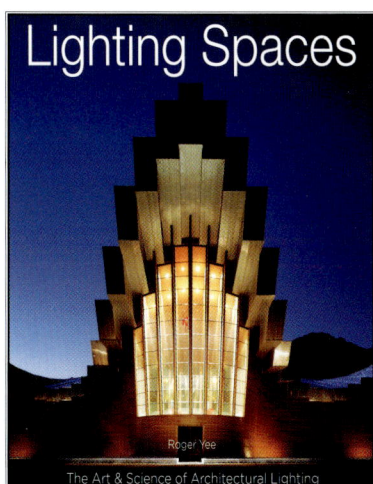

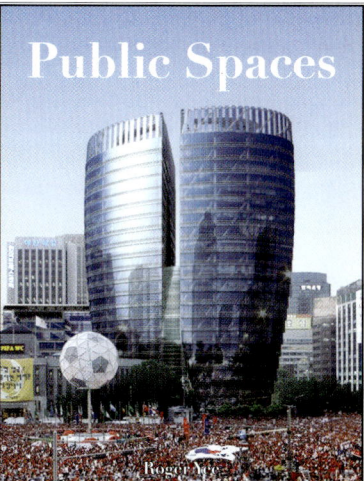

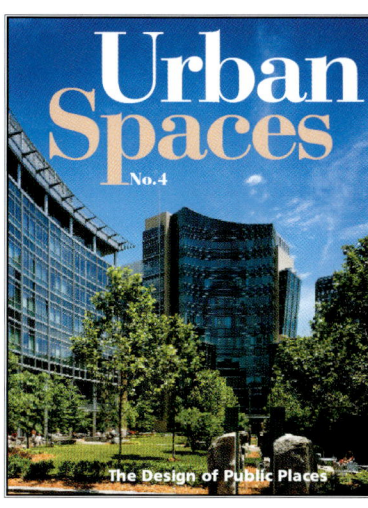

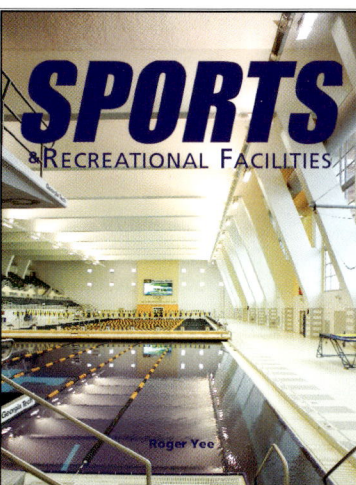

Advertisers Index